FORTRESS 111

# THE HINDENBURG LINE

**PATRICK R. OSBORN AND MARC ROMANYCH**
ILLUSTRATED BY ADAM HOOK

*Series Editor Marcus Cowper*

First published in Great Britain in 2016 by Osprey Publishing,
PO Box 883, Oxford, OX1 9PL, UK
1385 Broadway, 5th Floor, New York, NY 10018, USA
E-mail: info@ospreypublishing.com

A CIP catalogue record for this book is available from the British Library.

ISBN: 9781472814791
PDF e-book ISBN: 9781472814807
e-Pub ISBN: 9781472814814

Editorial by Ilios Publishing Ltd, Oxford, UK (www.iliospublishing.com)
Index by Alan Rutter
Typeset in Myriad Pro, Sabon and Helvetica Neue
Maps by Bounford.com
Artwork illustrations by Adam Hook
Originated by PDQ Media, Bungay, UK
Printed in China through World Print Ltd.

16 17 18 19 20 10 9 8 7 6 5 4 3 2 1

## ARTIST'S NOTE

Readers may care to note that the original paintings from which the color
plates in this book were prepared are available for private sale. The
Publishers retain all reproduction copyright whatsoever. The artist can be
contacted via the following email address:

Scorpio, 158 Mill Road, Hailsham, East Sussex BN27 2SH, UK
Email: scorpiopaintings@btinternet.com

The Publishers regret that they can enter into no correspondence upon this
matter.

## THE WOODLAND TRUST

Osprey Publishing are supporting the Woodland Trust, the UK's leading
woodland conservation charity, by funding the dedication of trees.

# CONTENTS

# THE HINDENBURG LINE

## INTRODUCTION

The Hindenburg Line, as it was known by the Allied armies, was the strongest defensive system built during World War I. Its reputation for impregnability was matched only by its ambitious design. Jagging across most of the Western Front in Belgium and northern France, nothing like it had ever been seen before. The extensive fortifications included deep zigzagging trench lines fortified with reinforced concrete shelters, heavily armed strongpoints and wide belts of barbed wire which combined to form an intimidating barrier for any attacking army and to maximize the firepower of war's two greatest killers – artillery and machine guns. The fortifications also skilfully integrated natural topographic features such as ravines, villages and waterways to afford every possible advantage to the defending troops and make any Allied advance as difficult and dangerous as possible. Perhaps its most ingenious use of terrain was turning parts of the St Quentin Canal into the world's largest anti-tank ditch. To drive the Germans from French soil, the Allies knew they had to overcome these obstacles – and it was a deadly task requiring new weapons and tactics.

Well-armed German infantry manning a forward position of the Wotan-Stellung near La Bassée in 1917. The German Army's strategy for the Western Front rested on using fewer troops entrenched in strong fortified positions to overcome Allied superiority in troops and firepower. (M. Romanych)

In 1917, the Hindenburg Line proved its purpose when major Allied offensives failed to break through the fortifications and end the defensive deadlock. However, despite the success of its defensive strategy, the German Army sowed the seeds of its own destruction by provoking the United States into declaring war while launching a series of offensives to end the war before the American Army could irrevocably tilt the military balance in the Allies' favour. In early 1918, the German Army abandoned the security of its fortification system to attack the Allies, but their logistical apparatus failed as they broke through Allied lines and left the Hindenburg Line behind. Suffering massive casualties in the process, by the end of summer, Allied counter-attacks threw German forces back to where they had started several months before and the Hindenburg Line became Germany's last line of defence. Only now, the army lacked the resources to defeat determined Allied attacks.

# CHRONOLOGY

## 1916

| | |
|---|---|
| **August** | Erich von Falkenhayn is replaced by Paul von Hindenburg and Erich Ludendorff at Oberste Heeresleitung (OHL), signalling a shift in German strategy to the defensive. |
| **September** | Ludendorff directs the army groups to study the feasibility of preparing two fortified withdrawal positions and initiates a doctrinal study that alters defensive operations and tactics for the remainder of the war. Construction commences on the first withdrawal position named the Siegfried-Stellung (Hindenburg Line). |

## 1917

| | |
|---|---|
| **16–20 March** | Operation *Alberich* – the German Army withdraws to the Siegfried-Stellung in anticipation of an Allied spring offensive. |
| **9 April–7 May** | During the battles of Arras and Bullecourt, the German Army's new defensive doctrine is put to the test against the British Expeditionary Force. |
| **16 April–9 May** | The German Seventh Army employs the army's new defensive doctrine to defeat a massive French offensive during the second battle of the Aisne (Nivelle Offensive). |
| **31 July–10 Nov** | In response to the British offensive during the third battle of Ypres, Army Group Crown Prince Rupprecht deepens the defences of the Flandern-Stellung. |
| **11 November** | The German High Command decides to launch a major offensive to defeat the British Army before American forces arrive in strength on the Western Front. |

| | |
|---|---|
| **20 Nov–7 Dec** | The first major Allied offensive against one of the fortified withdrawal positions is conducted by the British Third Army employing massed armour against the Siegfried-Stellung west of Cambrai. |

## 1918

| | |
|---|---|
| **21 March** | The German Army leaves the security of the Siegfried-Stellung during the first of its spring offensives on the Western Front. |
| **4 July** | During the battle of Hamel (near Amiens), the Australian Corps of the British Fourth Army successfully employs combined-arms tactics against entrenched German infantry. |
| **15 July** | The German Army launches its final offensive, dubbed the *Friedensturm* (Peace Offensive). |
| **18 July** | Franco-American forces launch a massive counter-attack, stopping the Peace Offensive. German forces remain on the strategic defensive until the end of the war. |
| **8–11 August** | During the battle of Amiens, British Fourth and French First armies employ the largest tank concentration of the war, inflicting a great defeat on the German Army and causing German troops to surrender in mass and shocking German military leaders. |
| **2–3 September** | The British First Army's Canadian Corps breaks through the Wotan-Stellung during the battle of the Drocourt–Quéant Line forcing the German Seventeenth Army to withdraw. |
| **26 Sept–16 Oct** | The US First Army and French Fourth Army attack in Champagne and the Meuse-Argonne pushing the German Third and Fifth armies back to the Kriemhild section of the Hunding-Stellung. |
| **27 Sept–1 Oct** | The British First Army crosses Canal du Nord and breaks through the Hagen-Stellung. It captures Cambrai a week later. |
| **29 Sept–3 Oct** | During the battle of the St Quentin Canal, the British Fourth Army seizes a 10-mile (16km) section of the Siegfried-Stellung. |
| **8 October** | The Siegfried-Stellung falls; Ludendorff orders the armies to withdraw to the Hermann-Stellung. |
| **25–26 October** | The British Fourth Army overruns the Hermann-Stellung followed by a French breach of the Hunding-Stellung. The German Army has no more fortified positions to withdraw to on the Western Front. |
| **11 November** | Germany agrees to an Armistice. |

# DESIGN AND DEVELOPMENT

The Hindenburg Line was the Allies' name for a series of strong, fortified defensive positions built by the Germans behind the front lines of the Western Front from 1916 to 1918. Though the name 'Hindenburg Line' was coined by the British in 1916 for the first such defensive line constructed by the Germans in the Somme region, the name was later expanded to encompass all rear area fortifications built by the German Army. The German name for the Hindenburg Line was the 'Siegfried-Stellung'. Siegfried was named after the main character from the Middle Ages German poem *Nibelungenlied* (*The Song of the Nibelungs*) and the word *Stellung* meant 'position', as in a defensive position. As the German Army built other similar fortified positions behind the front, the use of *Nibelung* character names (i.e. Michel, Wotan and Hunding) continued with but one exception, the Flandern-Stellung. The German Army often collectively referred to all five of its fortified positions as Siegfried-Stellungen (positions). By either name, the Hindenburg Line, or Siegfried-Stellung, was the most extensive fortification built by any army during World War I.

The origin of the Hindenburg, or Siegfried, fortifications lay in two major German defeats of 1916. First was the Fifth Army's offensive at Verdun that failed to weaken the French Army through attrition. The battle turned into a bloody six-month (February to July) stalemate that left both the German and French armies exhausted. Second was the Anglo-French offensive on the Somme that began in July and relentlessly wore down the German First and Second armies and slowly pushed the front line back to create a salient. These two lengthy and intense battles inflicted more than 700,000 casualties on the German Army, which also expended vast quantities of weapons and munitions, leaving it in a much weaker state relative to the British and French armies. Of the two battles, it was the Somme's alarming consumption of troops and material that put the greatest strain on the German Army and provided the impetus for change. Massive Allied artillery barrages had inflicted unimaginable carnage on the divisions of Heeresgruppe Kronprinz Rupprecht

The defences of the Siegfried and Wotan positions in the Somme and Flanders regions were the strongest and most complete. Two wide belts of barbed wire protect this well-built support trench east of Lens. Thinner belts protect each flank of the communications trench in the left centre. (NARA)

# German withdrawal positions, 1917–18

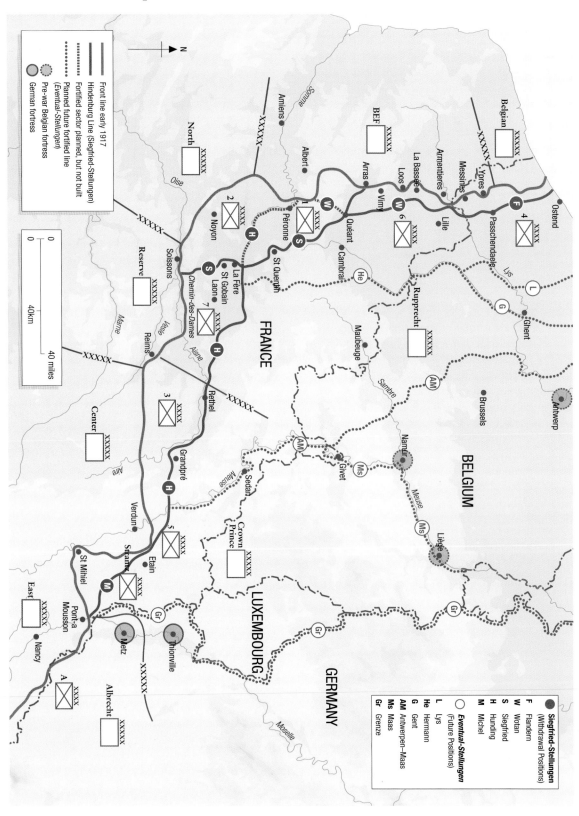

(Army Group Crown Prince Rupprecht). However, even as the battle dragged on and losses mounted, the senior German commander, Army Chief of the General Staff Erich von Falkenhayn, steadfastly insisted that units hold the front line at all costs and mount counter-attacks to regain ground lost to the Allies. This rigid strategy of holding terrain at the expense of men and material steadily depleted the front-line divisions and reserve formations.

By late August 1916, the deteriorating situation on the Western Front coupled with reverses in other theatres, led Kaiser Wilhelm II to replace Falkenhayn with Field Marshal Paul von Hindenburg, the famous commander of German forces on the Eastern Front. Along with Hindenburg came Lieutenant-General Erich Ludendorff, who assumed the second most senior position in the army, First Quartermaster General of the Oberste Heeresleitung (German High Command), or OHL. In this position Ludendorff would, among other duties, direct the operations of the German armies in the field. Upon assuming command, Hindenburg and Ludendorff immediately began forging a new strategy for the Western Front and on 8 September they convened a conference with senior army group and army leaders at Crown Prince Rupprecht's headquarters in Cambrai to review the situation. After much discussion, the assembled group concluded that the war had entered a dangerously destructive phase and that the operational initiative in the West was passing to the British and French armies. New strategy and tactics were needed to reduce casualties and material losses, otherwise the army would be drained of reserves and possibly collapse in the face of Allied offensive action in 1917.

Several important decisions came out of the Cambrai conference. First, the Fifth Army was ordered to cease attacks at Verdun and to release forces for employment on the Somme sector and the newly opened Romanian front. Next, Falkenhayn's order to hold the front line was rescinded to conserve manpower and restore defensive flexibility to the front-line divisions. Third, in anticipation of future Allied offensives, Ludendorff directed that the army groups study the feasibility of preparing two fortified *Rückzugsstellungen* (withdrawal positions) – one across the base of the Noyon salient from Arras

To conceal the construction of the Siegfried-Stellung from Allied intelligence, workshops, depots and other facilities were dispersed and camouflaged to prevent detection by aerial reconnaissance. (NARA)

Vast amounts of material were needed for the Siegfried fortified positions. This pile of screw pickets for the wire entanglements of the Michel-Stellung was located at Rembercourt-sur-Mad, about halfway between St Mihiel and Metz. (NARA)

to Laon and another across the base of the St Mihiel salient from Étain to Pont-à-Mousson. These fortifications eventually became known as the Siegfried-Stellung and Michel-Stellung respectively and were intended to shorten the length of the Western Front and release units for a reserve force. Although planning for the two positions was meant only as a precautionary measure, it did indicate a shift in Hindenburg and Ludendorff's strategy from the offence to the defence. In fact, the idea of building fortifications in the rear areas behind the front lines was conceived on the Eastern Front in 1915. The conference also initiated a doctrine review led by Ludendorff, which resulted in OHL issuing a series of documents in the last months of 1916 that altered the construction of fortifications, implemented new tactics and instituted organizational changes that determined how the army would conduct defensive operations for the remainder of the war.

Planning of the withdrawal positions proceeded quickly. Within two weeks, the staff of Army Group Crown Prince Rupprecht had sketched out the general course of the Siegfried-Stellung and begun initial coordination and preparations for construction. The proposed line of the defences ran from the existing front near Arras, south to St Quentin, past La Fère, and then rejoined the front east of Soissons. The position was sited well behind – up to 25 miles (40km) – the fronts of the First, Second and Seventh armies. In the north, the terrain was relatively featureless and offered no great advantage over the army group's current positions other than to reduce the length of front that would have to be defended. However, near the centre of the position, the city of St Quentin was integrated into the defences as a sort of fortified bastion, while along the southern half of the Siegfried-Stellung, the terrain was more distinct and provided several opportunities for strong defensive positions. There, the defences were sited to take advantage of the Oise River Valley north of La Fère and the forested heights in the area of St Gobain. Although this trace was significantly longer than the St Quentin–Laon–Reims line initially suggested by Ludendorff at the Cambrai conference, Army Group Crown Prince Rupprecht believed retaining the Chemin des Dames heights and the rail junction at Laon were tactical necessities even though so doing would create a salient in Allied lines at Soissons. The planned line of the Siegfried-Stellung was 88 miles (142km), which shortened the front by about 28 miles (45km) and was estimated to release eight to ten divisions with supporting troops and heavy artillery for employment elsewhere. OHL agreed with the army group's trace of the defences and on 27 September, Crown Prince Rupprecht ordered construction to commence with completion expected within five months.

While planning the Siegfried-Stellung, Army Group Crown Prince Rupprecht proposed construction of another withdrawal position to contain a possible Allied offensive between La Bassée and Arras. This position was located behind the 1915 battlefields of Loos, Vimy and Arras, along a 50-mile (80km) trace from east of Armentières to the northern shoulder of the Somme battlefield near Péronne. Named the Wotan-Stellung, the line crossed the Siegfried-Stellung at the town of Quéant. Unlike the Siegfried-Stellung, which was positioned well to the rear of the Somme battlefield, the Wotan-Stellung was located about only 10 miles (16km) behind the existing front line of the First and Sixth armies. While it did not appreciably shorten the front or conserve manpower, the new position did abandon the unfavourable boggy area around La Bassée. OHL approved the proposal on 4 November but, because labour and material were lacking, initiation of construction was set for after completion of the Siegfried-Stellung. Once both withdrawal positions were built, Army Group Crown Prince Rupprecht would have the option to either occupy the Wotan-Stellung and yield less ground, or abandon the Noyon salient and move back to Siegfried-Stellung in a larger, more strategic withdrawal. However, as it turned out, the army group withdrew to the Siegfried-Stellung in the spring of 1917 before construction of the Wotan-Stellung began and only the defences north of Quéant were built. Completion of the Wotan-Stellung extended the defences of the Siegfried-Stellung some 38 miles (61km) northwards to the area west of Lille and collectively the Wotan and Siegfried positions were often referred to by the British Army as the Hindenburg Line.

Temporary cement mixing plants and iron workshops such as this one in the Michel-Stellung were vital to the construction of concrete fortifications. A vast network of narrow-gauge railways was established to move materials to building sites. (NARA)

Meanwhile, in the Verdun sector, the staff of Heeresgruppe Deutscher Kronprinz (Army Group German Crown Prince) traced out the course of the Michel-Stellung. Part of a quiet front, the position was planned primarily to shorten the front and release divisions for employment elsewhere. The proposed line of defences was 37 miles (60km) long, almost half the distance of the current front line, and ran across the base of the St Mihiel salient in the sector of Armee-Abteilung Strantz (Army Detachment Strantz). The defensive positions were sited on high ground along a series of wooded ridgelines and hills and straightened the front enough to release up to five divisions from front-line duty. Although the Michel-Stellung was one of the two positions specifically proposed by Ludendorff during the Cambrai conference, the line was not scheduled for construction before the summer of 1917 because there were no indications of an impending French offensive in the region and any breakthrough by the French Army could be limited by the strong permanent fortifications located in the Metz–Thionville area.

The idea of rear area withdrawal positions was now firmly accepted by senior commanders and the army groups suggested several more withdrawal positions to OHL. Army Group Crown Prince Rupprecht proposed the Flandern-Stellung, a 45-mile (72km) position behind the Fourth Army in Flanders. The trace of this line was from the Belgian coast near Ostend, along the Passchendaele Ridge, behind the Messines salient, to the end of the Wotan-Stellung near Lille. Unlike the other planned withdrawal positions, the Flandern-Stellung was sited directly behind the current front line – about 6 miles (10km) away – and did not appreciably shorten the front. However, it did double the depth of the Fourth Army's defences and was viewed by OHL more as a deepening of existing front-line defences rather than a new rear area fortified position.

More ambitious was the 150-mile (241km) Hunding-Stellung planned in the sectors of the Second and Seventh armies of Army Group Crown Prince Rupprecht and the Third and Fifth armies of Army Group German Crown Prince Wilhelm. This line was situated to contain a French offensive against either the southern flank of the Noyon salient or the Champagne region. Its

The skilled labour used to perform concrete work was provided by German construction firms and army pioneer units. The *Feldmütze* (field caps) mark these men as pioneers. A wide belt of barbed wire is visible in the background. (M. Romanych)

trace stretched from Péronne to La Fère, behind the Picardy and Champagne battlefields of 1915, terminating near Étain north-east of Verdun where it linked to the Michel-Stellung. Because the line crossed the boundaries between two army groups, it was divided into sub-sections – the Brunhild-Stellung in the Picardy region behind the Second and Seventh armies and the Kriemhild-Stellung in the Champagne and Argonne regions behind the Third and Fifth armies. As planned, the position abandoned much more territory than the Siegfried-Stellung and gave up the Chemin des Dames and the important rail centres at La Fère and Laon. Its course ran from the southern end of the Wotan-Stellung near Péronne, along the Somme River to La Fère where it crossed the Siegfried-Stellung. This section, which was located in the area abandoned by the withdrawal to the Siegfried-Stellung, was never built. East of La Fère, the trace followed several river valleys and hill masses to Rethel and then Grandpré, to connect with the Michel-Stellung north of Verdun. Construction of the line was a low priority after the Siegfried, Wotan and Flandern positions opposite the British Army.

Withdrawal positions were also proposed behind the armies of Heeresgruppe Herzog Albrecht (Army Group Duke Albrecht) in Lorraine and Alsace. However, because this part of the front was stable and the modern fortifications at Strasbourg and older forts along the Rhine River already offered a defence against an Allied offensive, the withdrawal positions never got beyond the initial phases of planning.

By the end of 1916, five fortified positions were planned: Flandern, Wotan, Siegfried, Hunding and Michel. Once built, these positions formed a continuous fortified front from the Belgian coast to the Moselle River.

| Siegfried/Hindenburg Positions | | | | |
| --- | --- | --- | --- | --- |
| Position | Length | Army Sector | Initiation of Construction | Occupied |
| Flandern | 45 miles (72km) | 4th and 6th | June 1917 | August 1917 |
| Wotan | * Planned: 50 miles (80km) <br> Built: 45 miles (72km) | 6th and 1st | January 1917 | April 1917 |
| Siegfried | 88 miles (141km) | 6th, 1st, 2nd, and 7th | September 1916 | March 1917 |
| Hunding | * Planned: 150 miles (241km) <br> Built: 135 miles (217km) | 2nd, 7th, 3rd, 5th | March 1917 | November 1918 |
| Michel | 37 miles (60km) | Army Detachment Strantz | July 1917 | September 1918 |

* Note: The planned traces of the Wotan and Hunding positions were shortened after the German Army occupied the Siegfried-Stellung in March 1917.

## Building the Siegfried-Stellung

Although the order to build the Siegfried-Stellung was issued in late September 1916, construction did not commence immediately. The area under construction was exceptionally large – more than 500 square miles (1,400 square kilometres) – and nearly two months were needed to organize command and control, establish support infrastructure, lay out the defences and assemble materials and workers. At first, progress was hampered by the competing needs of civilian industry and the on-going Somme battle, but once the Allied offensive ended in early December 1916, work picked up pace despite continued shortages of manpower and material.

To manage the construction programme, a centralized command structure was established. At OHL, overall supervision was assigned to Colonel Kraemer, a staff engineer, and General Ludwig Lauter, the Inspector General of Artillery. On the ground, under direct command of OHL, specially designated construction staffs oversaw the building of the fortifications along specific sections of the Siegfried-Stellung. These construction staffs were formed from various entities to include reserve headquarters, dissolved commands and ad hoc groups of general staff officers. A typical construction staff was commanded by a general officer with a small group of artillery, engineer, machine gun and signal officers. These staff officers surveyed the assigned sector, sited the defensive positions, and managed the logistics of construction. Teams of geologists were provided to advise how to avoid ground water when deciding where to put trench lines and other field fortifications, where to excavate deep underground dugouts and where to find sand and gravel suitable for concrete work and road construction. Within the staff, a construction section directed the work of pioneer and labour companies assigned to the chief construction staff.

Building the fortifications required enormous amounts of labour and material. From October 1916 to March 1917, some 65–70,000 labourers worked on the fortifications. Many more labourers were used to build the fortifications of the other four withdrawal positions. The primary source of manpower was 50,000 Russian prisoners of war (POWs), even though under international law prisoners of war could not work on war-related activities. OHL also used 3,000 unemployed Belgian civilian workers as forced labour.

Iron reinforcement rods fashioned into a matrix gave concrete shelters their strength against artillery fire. This unfinished shelter in the Michel-Stellung – being inspected by American engineers after the war's end – has narrow-gauge railway tracks and turntables laid on top of the structure in preparation for pouring concrete. (NARA)

Belgian labourers pour the final layer of concrete over a shelter's reinforcement rods in the Brunhild section of the Hunding-Stellung north of Reims in July 1917. Thousands of Belgian civilians were forced into heavy labour by the German Army. (NARA)

Both groups of workers were organized into labour companies and given unskilled work such as digging entrenchments and earthworks. Twelve thousand troops from pioneer and reserve units and contracted civilians from German construction firms performed skilled labour for more complicated projects such as laying railway lines, building concrete emplacements and tunnelling dugouts. Material needs were equally huge. The concrete emplacements consumed most of the cement, sand and aggregate production of occupied France, Belgium and western Germany, as well as untold tons of lumber and steel. Significant quantities of gravel, sand and cement were also purchased from the Netherlands. To move the equipment, materials and personnel to the Siegfried-Stellung, some 50,000 standard-gauge railway cars (1,250 trains of 40 cars each) as well as 450 canal barges were used. To mix the cement needed for the fortifications, the German Army commandeered Belgian and French commercial cement works.

Construction followed an orderly sequence. First, the special construction staffs marked out the general line of the defences. Then the infrastructure – roads, railways, temporary workshops, goods depots, power stations and other life-support facilities – was put into place. The network of *Feldbahnen* (narrow-gauge field railways), for carrying building material and heavy equipment such as cement mixers to the vicinity of the construction sites, was important. As the required material and manpower arrived, construction of the concrete fortifications began, starting with the forward-most positions and moving rearward to the observation and command posts and artillery positions. To speed the concrete work, mass-production techniques were used, so the design of the various concrete fortifications was standardized as much as possible. Workshops produced pre-fabricated wood forms and sections of iron reinforcement rod that were transported to and assembled on site. Nearby cement works produced the concrete, which was brought to the building sites by narrow-gauge field railway. Once the forward fortifications were completed, the obstacle belts were emplaced, and, lastly, trenches and other earthworks were excavated.

### Withdrawal to the Siegfried-Stellung

Soon after work on the Siegfried-Stellung commenced, rumours circulated among German units that the army was preparing to retreat along the Western Front. In response, OHL issued an official statement in November disclaiming any intention to withdraw. Ludendorff was adamant that the front would be held until forced back by an Allied offensive, and he directed that work continue to strengthen the front-line defences of the Somme. However, as winter set in, the strategic situation did not improve. Germany's army was exhausted and nearly half of its divisions were tied down in the East, unavailable to reinforce the Western Front. The armaments industry struggled to produce the critical war material, especially ammunition, needed to recover from the battles of 1916. The British and French armies now had 40 divisions more than the German Army. With this situation in mind, Hindenburg and Ludendorff chose to remain on the defensive in the West while seeking victory in the East against Russia, while also endorsing an unrestricted submarine warfare campaign against Britain to weaken its economy – a policy that ultimately provoked the neutral United States to declare war.

By mid-January 1917, construction of the Siegfried-Stellung was progressing well despite delays imposed by cold weather. The position's forward trench system, obstacle belts and concrete works were finished while its second-line trench system, artillery observation posts and artillery positions were partially completed. Army Group Crown Prince Rupprecht considered its part of the Siegfried-Stellung to be defensible and, to strengthen the northern flank of the position, began construction along the southern half of the Wotan-Stellung. On 28 January, Crown Prince Rupprecht recommended to Ludendorff that the Siegfried-Stellung be occupied by mid-March before the Allies could launch their spring offensive. Ludendorff rejected the idea for political and strategic reasons, but directed OHL and the field commanders to consider other options such as a smaller-scale withdrawal to the Wotan-Stellung. However, none of the options solved the vexing problem of British and French numerical superiority. The only way to bolster the army before the next Allied offensive was by withdrawing to the Siegfried-Stellung, which would release 13 divisions from front-line duty and, just as importantly, free large quantities of munitions for redistribution to other divisions. With no viable alternative, Ludendorff gave the order on 4 February to accelerate work on the Siegfried-Stellung and to prepare for its occupation in five weeks. Construction work on the Wotan-Stellung was deferred until March and the workers and material were reallocated to the Siegfried-Stellung.

The withdrawal was codenamed Operation *Alberich* (named after the deceitful dwarf of the *Nibelungenlied*). Preparations began on 9 February. To impede the Allied advance into the evacuated area, OHL ordered the systematic removal or destruction of all material of military use. Towns and villages were razed, roads blocked by felled trees, crossroads cratered, railways torn up, bridges blown and wells destroyed. Most of the civilian population – some 125,000 people including the 45,000 inhabitants of St Quentin – were evacuated. As the army withdrew, a large number of mines, booby traps and delayed-action explosive charges were planted to cause casualties and delay the Allies. Security measures were taken to conceal construction of the Siegfried-Stellung and the preparations for withdrawal.

Reinforced concrete shelters were designed to withstand a direct hit from heavy artillery. This unfinished shelter for a trench mortar crew in the Kriemhild-Stellung features a roof 4 feet (1.2m) thick, a ventilation shaft and overhead camouflage. (NARA)

The backbone of the fortified positions were concrete shelters like this one built west of Cambrai behind the Siegfried-Stellung's main line of resistance. The shelter has a low profile to avoid targeting by artillery and is equipped with doors to protect occupants during a bombardment. Communication wires are visible crossing over the access trench. (NARA)

Although only partially effective, the measures kept British and French intelligence from learning the purpose of the Siegfried-Stellung or Operation *Alberich* until it was too late to prepare an effective response. British reconnaissance aircraft had first spotted the fortifications in November 1916. However, inclement weather, the use of screens and dummy works to hide construction and German control of the airspace hampered further air reconnaissance. Even information gleaned from German deserters and captured Russian prisoners of war was not enough to give Allied intelligence a complete or timely picture of German intentions.

Withdrawal of troops commenced on 16 March. Thirty-five divisions of the First, Second, Sixth and Seventh armies simultaneously pulled out of the front line, leaving one-third of their combat strength as a rear guard. Unprepared, the French and British armies were slow to pursue and no significant combat occurred. The withdrawal concluded four days later on 20 March, just 17 days before the Americans declared war. As German troops occupied the Siegfried-Stellung, they discovered that the defences were incomplete and in need of improvement and several weeks of work were required before it was an effective defensive position. Additionally, the organization of the defences did not closely follow the latest OHL doctrinal guidance. This gap between doctrine and reality occurred because most of the Siegfried-Stellung was planned before the new guidance could influence the layout and design of the defences. However, in one sense, the fortifications of all the withdrawal positions would never be entirely completed because they were repeatedly modified and rebuilt in response to new Allied weapons and tactics.

### Further construction

After the Siegfried-Stellung was occupied, construction of the Wotan-Stellung resumed with completion scheduled for the beginning of June. Work also proceeded on the Hunding-Stellung, followed in summer by the Flandern-Stellung and eventually the Michel-Stellung in the autumn. In 1918, plans were made to expand the Siegfried, Wotan and Flandern positions into deeper fortified zones by adding more trench systems, shelters and entanglements. As the new positions were planned and built, numerical designations – i.e. Siegfried I, II, II & IV; Wotan I, II, & III; and Flandern I & II – were given to differentiate the original and newer trench systems. Various switch positions were also built in the Flanders and Somme regions to connect the trench systems into networks, for example, Bayern in the Flandern-Stellung, and Hagen, Kanal and Otto in the Wotan-Stellung. In the Picardy, Champagne and Argonne regions intermediate, or reserve, fortified positions were planned for the area between the existing front line and the Hunding-Stellung, especially in the vicinity of Reims. The fortifications of these positions, named Ekkehard, Etzel, Giselher, Gudrun, Gunther, Hilldebrand, Mime, Perthes, Suippes, Volker,

Waldtraut, or simply Reserve 1 & 2 and Hauptwiderstandslinie 2, 3, & 4, were organized much like those of the Siegfried positions and, because they were built forward of the Hunding-Stellung, work was deferred on the Hunding position, especially along the Brunhild section, which became the rearmost in a series fortified positions. However, lacking time and resources, many of the additional positions were not fortified to the same degree as the Siegfried and Wotan positions and drew resources from construction of the Hunding and Michel positions, both of which were never completed. As the construction programme expanded, so did its material and labour requirements, and an estimated 370,000 soldiers, civilians and prisoners of war ultimately worked on these fortifications.

## Other defensive positions

Fortification building on the Western Front was not limited to just the Siegfried positions. In 1917, to defend against a British landing in the estuary of the Scheldt River, a 50-mile (80km) long position named the Holland-Stellung was constructed along the Belgian–Dutch border, from the sea coast to Antwerp, and the fortress at Antwerp was re-fortified by building concrete shelters and infantry positions along the outer ring of forts. The army also planned several new fortified withdrawal positions further behind the front. These positions, known as *Eventual-Stellungen* (future defensive positions), were intended as rallying positions if the army was pushed back towards Germany. Work was ordered on three of these positions, the Lys-Stellung, Gent-Stellung and Hermann-Stellung, on 12 September 1918. Together, they were to form a defensive position that stretched from the Belgian–Dutch border to the western end of the Hunding-Stellung; however, few defences were constructed. Another two future positions were planned further east. One, the Antwerpen–Maas-Stellung, went from Antwerp, through central Belgium and along the Meuse River, to the eastern end of the Hunding-Stellung near Verdun. The other, the Maas-Stellung, ran along the east bank of the Meuse River from the Dutch border north of Liège, south to Givet in France and included pre-war Belgian fortresses at Liège, and Namur. On 30 September 1918, OHL ordered work to commence on the Antwerpen–Maas-Stellung; however, it remained little more than a line on a map. In the event that the Allies threatened to invade Germany, OHL planned to build fortifications on the German border, called the Grenze-Stellung (border position), from Holland to Pont-à-Mousson in Lorraine, France. It also had modern, well-armed fortifications at Metz, Thionville and Strasbourg that it could use as strategic blocking positions against a wide-scale Allied offensive in Alsace and Lorraine. Finally, as a last-ditch defence, there were the 19th-century permanent fortifications guarding the Rhine River crossings at Wesel, Cologne (Köln), Koblenz, Mainz, Gemersheim, Neu Breisach and Istein.

A composite anti-tank barrier at Bernwiller. An American deception operation (the 'Belfort Ruse') was conducted in August 1918 to trick the Germans into believing an American attack would be launched toward Mulhouse and prompted the construction of a defensive position named the Hapsburg-Zone. (NARA)

# PRINCIPLES OF DEFENCE

German defensive doctrine developed through evolution rather than revolution. In late autumn 1914, as fighting in France and Belgium stalemated, OHL chief General Erich von Falkenhayn ordered the armies in the Western Front to go on the defensive. Insisting that the defensive posture did not signify a strategic defeat, Falkenhayn argued that the change was necessary to rest front-line troops and create reserves for future offensive operations. To emphasize the point, OHL retained exclusive authority to authorize any tactical withdrawals and placed trains on standby behind every army to deploy reserves rapidly across the front to respond to Allied attacks. After the first Allied offensive, the French attack in Champagne from December 1914 to March 1915, the German Army distributed a prescriptive analysis titled *Experiences Gained in the Winter Battle in Champagne*. The report, echoing measures already being taken in the field, indicated that siting front-line trenches on crests and forward slopes made them ideal targets for Allied artillery and concluded that the construction of reinforced shelters was necessary to protect soldiers and equipment. The report further stated that forward trenches were best located on a *Hinterhangstellung* (reverse slope) or in woods, to reduce their visibility to Allied observers, with saps leading to advanced machine gun and listening/observation posts. To counter enemy artillery, a second defensive line should be prepared approximately 1.5 miles (2.5km) behind the front-line trench system, ideally out of enemy sight, but close enough that machine guns could sweep the intervening ground. Forward positions were to consist of multiple closely spaced trenches and machine-gun positions emplaced in *Stützpunkte* (strongpoints) sited approximately every 1,000 yards (900m) along the front. Depending on the terrain, fighting positions – referred to as a *Zwischen-* or *Mittelstellungen* (intermediate positions) – could be placed between the first and second defensive lines and connected by communication trenches to allow the protected movement of troops.

The lessons drawn from the battle in the Champagne region were a significant departure from pre-war tactical instructions. The 1906 German

While German doctrine stressed avoiding forward-slope defences, these small, concealed concrete shelters near Prény in the Michel-Stellung were set in a checkerboard pattern to give depth to the position and prevent Allied gunners from firing on all of them at once. (NARA)

infantry manual prescribed construction of a single defensive line to concentrate rifle fire against approaching enemy troops and described rearward strongholds only as places to gather reserves. The manual also forbade the creation of advanced posts, since their inevitable loss to enemy attackers would drain morale. Now, where terrain permitted, the *Experiences* document called for advanced strongpoints to be built 800–1,000 yards (700–900m) in front of trenches so that they could fire on enemy formations before they could reach the front line. The utility of the concept was proven during a surprise British attack at Neuve Chapelle in March 1915, which successfully punched a mile-wide (1.5km) hole in the German front line, but was delayed by flanking fire from a few defending machine guns in advanced strongpoints until additional Germans troops arrived and prevented a breakthrough.

Entanglement belts such as these near Warq in the Michel-Stellung were sited to delay attacking infantry and channel them into pre-planned machine-gun crossfire. (NARA).

Despite his overall strategic defensive stance, Falkenhayn, in accordance with German military tradition, steadfastly ordered front-line divisions to launch *Gegenstöße*, or immediate counter-attacks to regain any ground lost to Allied attacks before their troops had time to consolidate and prepare a defence. Critical to the success of a *Gegenangriff* (counter-attack) was the ability of strongpoints to hold out until the counter-attack occurred, and for reserve formations to counter-attack before the enemy's artillery could move forward to shell German rear trenches and counter-attack units. Ideally, the counter-attacks would be launched from positions close enough to the enemy that its supporting artillery could not bombard the counter-attacking formations without also shelling their own troops. To generate overwhelming firepower, trenches captured by the enemy were to be attacked simultaneously from the flanks and front, placing them in a heavy crossfire. Heavy fighting in the Champagne region also prompted front-line units to construct many additional non-standardized field fortifications and switch trenches to facilitate defensive crossfire and constrict French attempts to break through one trench line in order to outflank another.

In October 1915 OHL issued *Gesichtspunkte für den Stellungskrieg (Aspects of Position Warfare)* which reinforced the points made in *Experiences* and again instructed units to fortify the front line and then hold it at all costs. A typical front-line position consisted of two or more parallel trench lines dug 110–165 yards (100–150m) apart. Bunkers and shelters were built into the trench lines for protection against heavy artillery and wide belts of barbed-wire entanglements up to 33 yards (30m) deep were placed in front of the first trench line to impede the enemy's advance. By the summer of 1916, some sectors in the Flanders and Somme regions had two or three belts of entanglements. The second, or reserve trench, system was similar but less fortified, creating a layered defensive position as much as 2.5 miles (4km)

Late-war German defensive doctrine emphasized superior artillery observation over the battle zone. American officers surveying German defences after the Armistice encountered a wide variety of creatively designed observation towers. This example was over 60 feet (18m) tall. (NARA)

deep. However, despite the increasing depth of the defences, tactics remained focused on preventing the loss of the front line. To repel an Allied attack, the forward trenches were fully manned while the second trench system was occupied by units positioned in reserve who would be used to contain a breakthrough or mount a counter-attack to retake lost positions. The primary purpose of the rearward positions was to provide cover for reinforcements and only when necessary serve as a fallback position for troops pushed out of the front-line trenches until a counter-attack was launched. Artillery batteries were emplaced close behind the second trench system from where they could fire on trenches opposite German lines and yet be far enough to the rear to avoid concentrated enemy artillery fire. Additional OHL instructions specified that the batteries would be assigned specific bombardment zones in no man's land into which they would fire a concentrated but brief pre-planned *Sperrfeuer* (blocking) barrage during an enemy attack. This mid-war concept of forward defence focused on holding and retaking ground rather than destroying the enemy force or reducing casualties among the defending troops. In contrast, Falkenhayn's emphasis on launching an immediate counter-attack played into the hands of the Allies, whose artillery and automatic weapons inflicted enormous casualties among counter-attacking troops.

As casualties mounted during the battle of Verdun in early 1916, Falkenhayn finally realized that densely held front-line trenches led to heavy casualties, and that the number of soldiers holding the front line should be thinned during preparatory barrages. However, he still demanded that units conduct counter-attacks to recapture lost terrain even though doing so resulted in an enormous number of casualties. In a vain attempt to reduce losses, Falkenhayn ordered that immediate, hasty counter-attacks be replaced

## A SECTION OF THE SIEGFRIED-STELLUNG

After the battle of the Somme, the German Army's new doctrine reorganized defences along the Western Front from a thinly held fortified line to a deep zone of semi-permanent fortifications. This regiment-sized sector of the Siegfried-Stellung (Hindenburg Line) near the village of Quéant demonstrates how the fortifications were organized into a zone defence. Closest to Allied lines was the outpost zone consisting of listening and observation posts loosely arrayed into an early-warning security line. Behind were rudimentary earthworks (F) occupied by assault teams for countering Allied patrols and raids. Manning the outpost zone were squad- and platoon-sized elements from battalions holding the main line of resistance. If a major Allied ground attack occurred, troops in the outpost zone withdrew to the main line to rejoin their battalions. The main line of resistance, located on a reverse slope, was a complex system of trenches fronted by belts of wire entanglements designed to blunt and break the cohesion of an Allied attack. Interspersed within the trench system were concrete shelters to protect troops against artillery fire, along with

machine-gun positions, strongpoints (S), trench-mortar positions and more wire entanglements. To the rear of the trench system was the battle zone where fighting positions and strongpoints manned by battalion reserves and machine-gun companies (R) were sited to hold or delay Allied penetrations while observation posts directed artillery fire on Allied troops in the outpost zone, main line of resistance and battle zone. Switch trenches (T) were built as flanking positions for containing an Allied advance through the battle zone. The last line of defence was the artillery protective line located at the rear edge of the battle zone. This line consisted of a second system of trenches and wire entanglements located on a reverse slope so as not to be visible from the battle zone. Manning the artillery protective line was the regiment's reserve battalion, positioned to prevent Allied formations from penetrating further and to act as the vanguard of a counter-attack. The regiment headquarters (H) and the forward-most artillery positions (A) were located behind the artillery protective line, in the rearward zone.

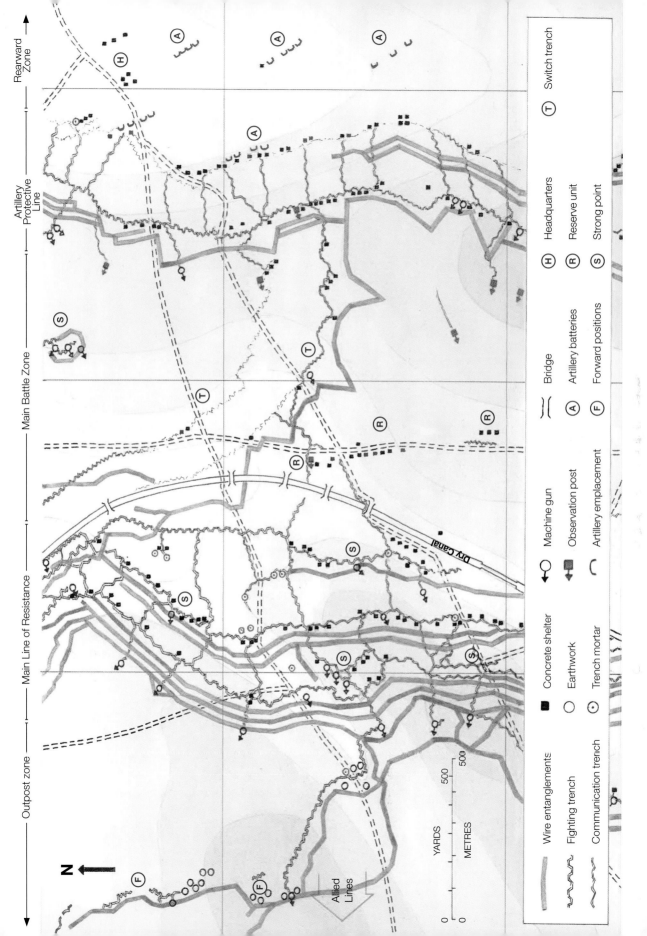

N

Outpost zone ——|—— Main Line of Resistance ——|—— Main Battle Zone ——|—— Artillery Protective Line ——|—— Rearward Zone

Allied Lines

Dry Canal

YARDS

METRES

500

500

0

0

| | | |
|---|---|---|
| ~ Wire entanglements | ■ Concrete shelter | ⌀ Machine gun |
| ~ Fighting trench | ○ Earthwork | ▨ Observation post |
| ~ Communication trench | ⊙ Trench mortar | ⊂ Artillery emplacement |

| | | |
|---|---|---|
| )( Bridge | Ⓗ Headquarters | Ⓣ Switch trench |
| Ⓐ Artillery batteries | Ⓡ Reserve unit | |
| Ⓕ Forward positions | Ⓢ Strong point | |

After the battle of the Somme the German Army stopped constructing fortified artillery positions. Instead, to avoid increasingly deadly Allied counter-battery fire, the guns often relocated to pre-prepared earthwork positions sited in shallow ravines or a stand of trees for concealment. (NARA)

with deliberately planned attacks supported by artillery. However, these half-measures were not enough to solve the German Army's impending problem of personnel and material shortages. The experiences of the German First and Second armies during the battle of the Somme clearly demonstrated the need for a revision of the 1915 doctrine. During the preliminary bombardment of the offensive, Allied guns fired nearly two million shells, collapsing German front-line trenches and dugouts, which were within range of Allied artillery, visible from Allied lines, and spaced too close together. Even the deepest and most well-constructed dugouts and shelters were destroyed, inflicting heavy casualties among the densely packed front-line infantry companies. Reports from the front often used the term 'obliterate' to describe the effect of bombardment by Allied heavy artillery. To counter the destructive power of the Allied guns, front-line divisions and regiments learned to reduce the number of troops in the forward trenches and disperse units to present fewer concentrated targets to massed artillery attacks. These emerging tactics invalidated the principles of forward defence and presaged the concept of in-depth defence.

## New defensive doctrine

After Hindenburg replaced Falkenhayn in August 1916, new defensive doctrine was developed under Erich Ludendorff's direction by combining OHL staff concepts with lessons learned from units in the field. In their own ways, both groups were moving towards the idea of defence in depth. At OHL, Colonel Max Bauer and Captain Hermann Geyer of the operations section worked on a new theory of defence largely based on concepts borrowed from a French Army document captured in May 1915 describing a flexible or elastic type of defence in depth based on strongpoints organized into defensive zones. Lessons learned were extracted from unit reports and combined with ideas and opinions solicited by Ludendorff during a series of field visits. Colonel Friedrich ('Fritz') von Lossberg, chief of staff of the Second Army, who was sceptical of discarding the idea of holding ground regardless of cost, proved particularly influential in the development of the doctrine after he eventually converted to Bauer's and Geyer's point of view. The result of this collaborative effort was a series of documents that codified and implemented the concept of defence in depth and shifted the focus of defensive operations from holding terrain to the methodical destruction of attacking enemy forces. Lossberg would soon become OHL's defensive warfare fireman, taking charge of operations on various parts of the Western Front when crises developed and was instrumental in implementing OHL doctrine.

The first of OHL's new doctrinal documents, *Allgemeines über Stellungsbau* (*Basic Principles of the Construction of Field Positions*), was

published on 13 November 1916 and quickly followed by *Grundsätze für die Führung in der Abwehrschlacht im Stellungskrieg* (*Basic Principles for the Conduct of Defensive Battle in Position Warfare*) on 1 December. These documents altered the structure of defensive positions from a thin, strongly held fortified line to a deep-zone defence with dispersed fortified positions. They also provided instructions for organizing defences in a way that required fewer troops, reduced casualties and used terrain to set favourable conditions for battle. *Basic Principles* described an idealized defensive system consisting of three successive defensive zones – outpost, battle and rearward – that together formed a defensive position up to 9 miles (14km) deep. This deepening of the defences created a defensive zone more than three times the depth of previous fortified areas. Each zone had its own tactical purpose and organization. Closest to the enemy front line was the outpost zone, intended to prevent enemy patrolling into the battle zone and provide early warning of raids and attack. Reducing the number of troops manning this area helped reduce the number of casualties inflicted by enemy long-range weapons. Located behind the outpost zone was the battle zone, though, depending on terrain, the outpost and battle zones could be merged into one another. Some German commanders, such as Crown Prince Rupprecht, actually objected to the use of the term 'outpost' on the grounds that inexperienced or weaker-willed soldiers would be quick to retire from these positions if they perceived they were not intended to hold out indefinitely. As most front-line troops were regarded as expendable, the term, while used in OHL documents, was omitted from lower-level tactical issuances.

The battle zone was the area in which an attacking enemy force would be decisively engaged. Behind the battle zone was the rearward zone, designed to delay an enemy force breaking through the battle zone. To prevent a simultaneous artillery attack on all the defences, the rearward zone was located well back from the front of the battle zone, out of range of all but the heaviest Allied artillery. Intelligent use of terrain was integral to the zone concept, particularly the use of reverse-slope positions for the outpost and main battle zones as cover and concealment from enemy direct-fire weapons and observed artillery fire. The establishment of long defensive fields of fire was considered secondary to the need to hide from Allied artillery observation.

When possible, water obstacles were integrated into defences to hinder both infantry and tanks. Wire entanglements were added to this man-made inundation in the Michel-Stellung. Similar defences were encountered by Allied troops a generation later, most notably in Normandy. (NARA)

To facilitate quick action, firing positions were built immediately adjacent to the concrete shelters. This abandoned machine-gun position in the Kriemhild-Stellung, its walls shored on one side by wattle, exhibits signs of heavy action such as being struck by mortar rounds. (NARA)

The *Basic Principles* also emphasized integrating terrain and man-made features such a villages, quarries and sunken roads into the defences. Indeed, supporting positions throughout the battle zone were to be staggered and as irregular as possible to prevent simultaneous bombardment by Allied artillery. Strongpoints were complemented by 'holding points' which were smaller fighting positions prepared in shell holes, thick vegetation such as hedgerows, or other convenient concealed spots for use during delaying actions against Allied penetrations and for protecting withdrawing troops or formations gathering for counter-attacks. The intent was for units to establish a wide range of weak positions rather than rely on a small number of strong ones upon which Allied formations could focus their firepower. Weaker manning of fighting positions ran counter to traditional practice, but *Basic Principles* emphasized that it was not numerical superiority but inter-arms cooperation, quick thinking and prompt action that were the keys to success.

Two trench systems separated the three defensive zones: the *Hauptverteidigungslinie* (main line of resistance) located between the outpost and main battle zone and the *Artillerieschutzstellung* (artillery protective line) located between the main battle and rearward zone. The main line of resistance was the forward edge of the battle zone and it was typically the most fortified part of the defensive zone. As implied by its name, the purpose of the artillery protective line was to protect the artillery and to allow its withdrawal in case of an Allied breakthrough of the main battle zone. To promote a flexible defence, the structure of the trench systems was changed from two continuous and parallel trench lines into a network of irregularly

## B  ENTANGLEMENTS AND TRENCHES

This 670-yard (600 m) section of the Wotan-Stellung, near Douai, typifies the fortifications constructed during the winter and spring of 1917. The principal strengths of the fortifications were the wire entanglements and trenches. Forward of the first trench line lay several belts of entanglements **(1)**, each about 33 feet (10m) wide and densely packed with barbed wire. Intervals separated the belts to make them difficult to breach with artillery fire. Behind the belts were irregular-shaped blocks of wire **(2)** designed to channel attacking Allied infantry into the crossfire of machine guns positioned in the first trench line. Wire entanglements were of two different heights: 'high entanglements' set to chest level (up to 4 feet or 1.2m) to form an impassable barrier to infantry and 'low entanglements' **(3)** strung at waist height (about 2.5 feet or 0.75m) to provide a clear field of fire for machine guns. Field works **(4)** for forward observation posts and machine-gun emplacements were dug in among the entanglements. The forward-most trench **(5)** was constructed

with alternating fire-bays and traverses along most of its length. Concrete shelters **(6)** were emplaced at regular intervals in the trench lines and protected soldiers from artillery bombardment. Communication trenches **(7)** provided protection for the movement of troops and supplies in and out of the forward trench line. Intermediate trenches **(8)** connected shelters for machine guns, trench mortars and headquarters and served as alternative fighting positions. Entanglements **(9)** erected behind the first trench line were narrower (about 15 feet or 4.5m) and less dense than the forward belts. Gaps in the entanglements of the rearward belt permitted the passage of troops. Another trench line **(10)**, also reinforced with concrete shelters, was located some 100–200 yards (90–180m) further back to serve as a second line of defence and support trench for repositioning soldiers behind the front line. With time, units occupying the sector built additional entanglements, trenches and fighting positions.

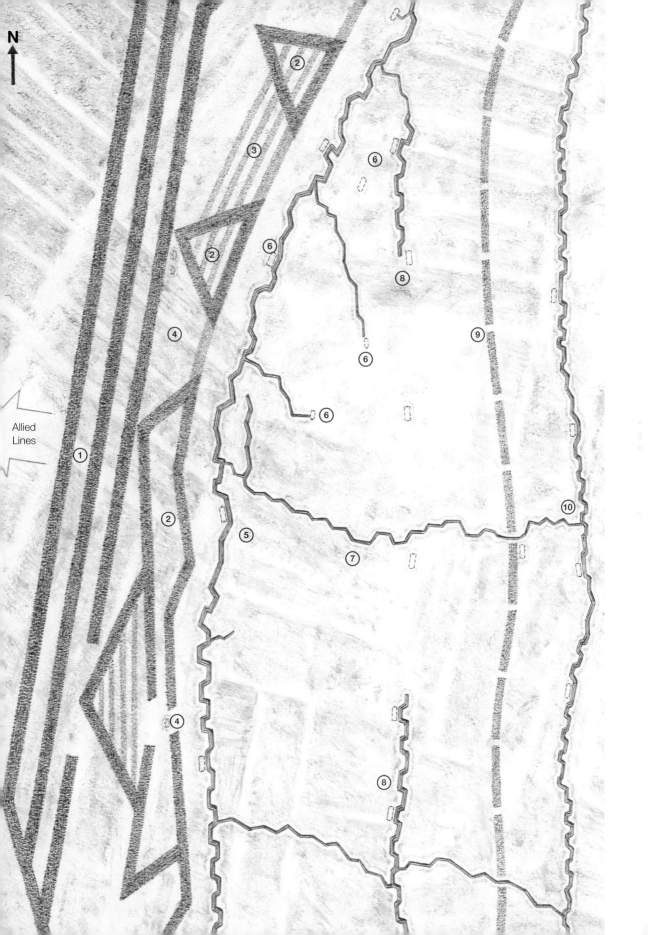

N

Allied
Lines

②

②

③

②

④

①

②

④

⑥

⑥

⑥

⑤

⑦

⑥

⑧

⑨

⑩

⑧

Extensive wattle in this well-constructed Kriemhild-Stellung trench in the Meuse-Argonne indicates that it had been occupied for years before being overrun by American troops in 1918. (NARA)

and wider-spaced entrenchments interconnected by communication and approach trenches which units could use to move about the defensive zones to counter enemy action. Built into the trench systems and defensive zones were various dugouts, shelters, weapons positions and observation posts organized into mutually supporting unit-sized strongpoints. Central elements of the defence were machine gun emplacements and artillery observation posts, sited throughout the defensive zones to create overlapping fields of machine-gun fire and concentrated artillery fire. Belts of wire entanglements channelled enemy attacks into interlocking fields of fire and blocked assaults on the trenches and fighting positions.

The new doctrine altered tactics too. *Basic Principles* declared that more than 50 per cent of defending troops should be positioned behind the battle zone for immediate or small-scale prepared counter-attacks. Every soldier was to be imbued with the idea that stubborn resistance was critical to defeating enemy incursions and, if surrounded, small groups and even individual soldiers were expected to resist to the last. *Eingreif* (intervention or interference) divisions were to be kept on standby nearby, ready to move forward and conduct large-scale deliberate counter-attacks against enemy penetrations of the battle zone at the moment when enemy formations were exhausted from fighting through the forward defences and fresh German reserves were assembled in position for the attack. The famous German soldier Ernst Jünger likened this arrangement to a net into which the enemy would be snagged, only to be annihilated by concentrated firepower. The challenge for German commanders was to time the counter-attack to hit the enemy force at its most vulnerable moment.

To minimize losses to artillery fire, forward area fighting positions were small, shallow field entrenchments that were difficult to observe and target with artillery. The forward infantry companies were expected to abandon these positions when under intense bombardment, with the infantry in the outpost zone moving forward into no man's land to occupy *Trichterstellungen* (shell-hole positions). Counter-intuitively, many troops preferred open-air positions instead of remaining in claustrophobic shelters where they might be buried alive. The irregularity of shell holes reduced target concentration for enemy weapons and further enhanced crossfire in the outpost zone. Further to the rear, more elaborate entrenchments and shelters were constructed to survive fire from long-range heavy artillery, and communications trenches were prepared to allow troop movement during bombardment. To mitigate Allied ground and aerial reconnaissance, concealment and camouflage of the fortifications was also deemed necessary, while dummy positions were built to draw artillery fire and air-to-ground aircraft attacks away from real targets. The growing effectiveness of Allied aircraft to direct artillery fire and strafe troop concentrations was another reason to thin defences and assign more anti-aircraft weapons to the forward areas.

Along with changes to fortifications and tactics, the doctrine also prompted several operational and organization changes to increase combat effectiveness of front-line units. Most significantly, the frontage defended by each division was reduced. This not only expanded the depth of terrain defended by each division and encouraged the creation of local reserves, but it also facilitated familiarity with the ground and communication among companies and battalions as they rotated between forward, battle and rear areas. To improve fire support to front-line troops, divisions received a heavy mortar section and control over its own heavy artillery. At the company level, firepower was increased to six light machine guns and six light trench mortars, and small unit flexibility was improved by making the eight-man squad, rather than the company itself, the basic combat unit. Oddly, anti-tank measures were absent from the new doctrine even though the first British tanks were encountered on the Somme in September 1916. OHL, apparently unimpressed by the British tanks, did nothing, even though a department in the War Ministry was directed to design a tank for the army, the plans of which were unveiled in December 1916.

Dummy guns, like this one in the Michel-Stellung, were built to draw the attention of Allied aerial reconnaissance away from actual artillery. Phoney wooden tanks were also built to fool Allied observers as to the location of reserve and counter-attack forces. (NARA)

## Application of the doctrine

The new doctrine was put to the test during three major Allied offensives in April and May 1917, although the fortifications of the withdrawal positions were attacked only once. The first offensive – the battle of Arras – began on 9 April 1917 when three British armies attacked German lines east of Arras in a sector where the doctrine had been largely ignored by officers of the Sixth Army who, steeped in the old ways of doing things, had refused to adopt the new concepts and tactics. This failure allowed British forces, who themselves had new weapons and tactics, to break the front line and advance 3 miles (5km) towards the Wotan-Stellung. The defending German divisions suffered high losses in the front-line trenches and, unable to mount counter-attacks, could only fall back until the British advance bogged down. Furious at the Sixth Army's poor performance, Ludendorff angrily demanded prompt implementation of the defensive doctrine and dispatched Lossberg to rearrange and energize German defences as chief of staff to Sixth Army. When the British renewed the offensive a few days later on 14 April, Lossberg deftly executed a flexible defence. Front-line troops slowly gave ground as artillery slowed the British first wave and separated it from the creeping barrage and follow-on formations. The British troops, expecting their barrage to neutralize German defences, instead found themselves under intense small-arms fire from reverse slope positions and vulnerable to counter-attack. Within hours, the Germans had stopped the British troops and then pushed them back to their start line. The action at Arras convinced Lossberg that the doctrine was sound and the key to success was its proper application. Smaller

Over the course of the war Allied photo interpretation became more effective at detecting German camouflage efforts. Fake defences were often built to mislead Allied intelligence and misdirect artillery bombardments. (NARA)

diversionary actions just south-east of Arras (the first launched against the Siegfried-Stellung proper) reinforced confidence in the new methods. At Bullecourt, near the junction of the Wotan and Siegfried positions, poor weather and lack of infantry–tank coordination spoiled an attack by I ANZAC (Australian and New Zealand Army Corps) on 11 April. Slightly larger efforts in May managed to capture a short section of the Siegfried-Stellung, but the Australian 4th Division suffered heavy casualties at the hands of the Württemberg 27th Infantry Division, which had recently served as a demonstration unit training other units in the new doctrine.

Next was the second battle of the Aisne, also known as the Nivelle Offensive. Planned as a war-winning offensive by French commander-in-chief Robert Nivelle, the attack began on 16 April with the two French armies attacking along a broad front between Soissons and Reims. The defending German Seventh Army was entrenched in strong fortified positions that dated back to late 1914 and had been continually expanded and improved since, but it was not physically organized according to OHL's new doctrine. However, the tactics used by the Seventh Army were based on the new

## C CONSTRUCTION OF A CONCRETE SHELTER

Concrete shelters were built in an assembly-line manner. Construction began by excavating a large, square hole for the shelter (1) to fit the outside dimensions of the shelter. Three sides of the hole were cut vertically so that concrete could be poured directly against the ground without the use of forms. The fourth side of the hole was shaped with a step or shelf that became the access trench to the rear of the shelter. When excavation was completed, either a tiled drain or sump drainage system was installed. The next stage of construction was the installation of the forms and reinforcement rods (2). Pre-fabricated wood forms and sections of iron reinforcement rod were made in nearby workshops and then fitted and assembled by workmen on site. The wood forms were used to create interior spaces, entrance ways and the rear facade of the shelter, while the ceiling of the

interior space was lined with sheets of corrugated iron and the entrance ways were topped with L-beams. The reinforcement rods were embedded in the shelter's concrete floors, walls and ceiling. The reinforcement generally consisted of ¾-inch (2cm) rods spaced every foot (30cm) or so into a 3-dimensional mesh. Once the forms and reinforcement rods were in place, a narrow-gauge railway was laid across the top of the structure in preparation for pouring concrete (3). Made in a nearby mixing plant, the concrete was brought to the work site in narrow-gauge railway dump cars and poured from the tracks into the forms. The concrete was poured in layers and allowed to cure. To complete the shelter, the forms were removed and earth was backfilled over the top of the shelter. Any remaining earth was spread out and covered with grass sod (4).

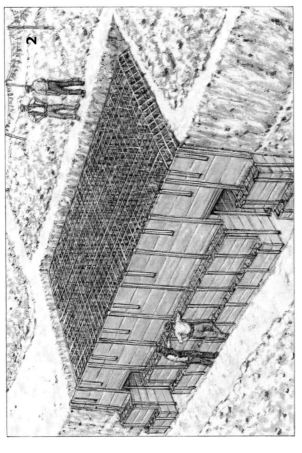

1

2

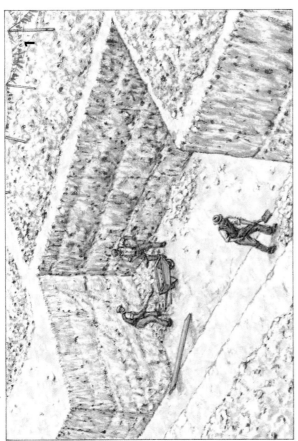

3

4

doctrine and on the first day, closely spaced machine-gun positions decimated French infantry under intense crossfire while artillery pounded the formations with devastating effect. The German success was greatly aided by the French Army's poor use of artillery and a breakdown in discipline and morale. The result was more than 40,000 French casualties and the loss of dozens of tanks in a French debacle – another validation of OHL's defensive tactics. However, the offensive continued on into early May and the French Sixth Army eventually gained more ground and a short section of the southern end of the Siegfried-Stellung that was abandoned when the German Seventh Army withdrew to shorten its front line.

The third offensive, known as the third battle of Ypres or Passchendaele, was launched by two British armies in Flanders on 31 July. The attack was preceded by a ten-day preliminary bombardment that warned the defending German Fourth Army of the impending attack. Concerned, Crown Prince Rupprecht proposed a withdrawal to the uncompleted Flandern-Stellung, the construction of which had only begun the month before. However, Lossberg, now the chief of staff of Fourth Army, rejected the idea and ordered that the current front line – now designated Flandern I – be held as the forward position of the Flandern-Stellung, while work on Flandern II and another position named Flandern III was completed. Desperately seeking to break through German lines, the British engaged in a costly battle of attrition that featured devastating heavy artillery bombardments during wet weather that turned the battlefield into a quagmire. Employing innovative offensive methods based upon mixed weapons platoons of riflemen, grenadiers and Lewis gunners using fire and movement, helped British troops capture Flandern I fortifications. Although the German Fourth Army inflicted high casualties on the attackers, to cope with British artillery it had to adapt doctrine by further dispersing troops in forward positions, moving reserve battalions behind the artillery protective line and increasing counter-battery fire to reduce British artillery fire. Finally, after more than three months of battle, the British captured Flandern I, only to face two more deeply fortified defensive positions. The German Army could not afford the casualties it had suffered, and the stage was set for another change of German strategy on the Western Front.

## ORGANIZATION OF A DEFENSIVE POSITION

Although all five fortified withdrawal positions were planned and constructed according to the same doctrinal principles, none achieved the doctrinal ideal, and the organization of defences within the positions varied from one sector to another because of adaptations to local topography. By far the strongest defences were built in the Siegfried and Wotan positions. The low rolling hills of the region were ideal for organizing successive defensive lines into a deep battle zone. Especially strong were the defences constructed between Cambrai and St Quentin, which were designed to halt a massive British offensive. The Wotan-Stellung, which was essentially an extension of the Siegfried-Stellung's northern flank, was similarly heavily fortified. Further north, Flandern-Stellung defences were enhanced by reinforcing and deepening the existing front line, turning it into a hybrid defensive zone that combined older pre-1917 with newer 'Siegfried-type' fortifications. Opposite the French Army in Picardy, whole sections of fortifications on both the Brunhild and Kriemhild

Barbed wire was lavishly used to build wide, dense entanglement belts that could withstand prolonged Allied bombardments. The blast that created the foreground crater only increased the jumble, so the Allies fitted shells with sensitive contact fuses that could destroy wire without cratering. (IWM)

portions of the Hunding-Stellung were not completed, although the rough terrain of the Argonne did not require extensive fortifications to be defendable. Lastly, the Michel-Stellung, one of the two original withdrawal positions directed for study by General Ludendorff, was, ironically, the weakest of the lot because it was located in a quiet sector of the front and it did not receive construction priority until the last few months of the war.

The fortifications of the withdrawal positions consisted of four primary elements – wire entanglements to contain or slow down attacking infantry, trenches to provide fighting positions, concrete shelters and dugouts to protect soldiers from artillery fire, and observation posts and gun emplacements for the employment of artillery. In the war's final year, another element – tank defence – was added in response to the Allies' use of tanks. The details of these elements – particularly the shelters – varied significantly from sector to sector. This was partly due to differences in building materials and methods but also because the design of the fortifications evolved in response to new weapons and tactics, so the date of construction was also significant in terms of the physical design and layout of the defences.

A fighting trench in the Siegfried-Stellung near Cambrai. Its rough construction reflects a lack of resources for maintaining hundreds of miles of trenches and a de-emphasis on holding ground regardless of cost. The parados' high bank enhanced the trench's anti-tank effect. (IWM)

This narrow Siegfried-Stellung sap connects a distant forward position to the main trench line. Barbed wire on each side hindered Allied troops from entering the trench, while its winding course limited the effects of enfilade fire and artillery shelling. (IWM)

## Wire entanglements

Broad belts of barbed-wire entanglements were emplaced forward of the fortified positions to slow an Allied attack. The trace of the entanglements followed an irregular path, zigzagging in front of the trenches to provide fields of fire for machine guns. Additional entanglements were placed throughout the battle zone between trench systems, along communication trenches and around strongpoints to limit the advance of any infantry that penetrated the forward defences. In some sectors of the Siegfried and Wotan positions, the entanglement belts were up to 100 feet (30m) wide, but elsewhere belts of about 33 feet (10m) wide were typical. To increase the depth of the entanglements, a third belt of wire was added or irregular-shaped blocks of entanglements were emplaced to divide and channel attacking formations of infantry into machine-gun fire. The intervals between the belts were sometimes filled with wire set at ankle height to trip attacking infantry or pointed iron stakes to injure them. Entanglements erected further to the rear of the battle zone were not as wide – perhaps only 16 feet (5m) – or as dense as the forward belts. As the strength of front-line units was depleted, the fortified positions featured more and more barbed wire, taxing German industry's ability to produce it.

## D  TYPICAL CONCRETE SHELTER

Concrete shelters served as the backbone of the Siegfried Line fortifications, enabling the infantry to hold forward trench lines during intense Allied artillery bombardment. A typical front-line shelter measured only 30 feet (9m) long and 14 feet (4m) wide with 3-feet (1m) thick walls and a 4-feet (1.2m) thick roof. The shelter had two entrances (1), which were recessed and separated from the interior by baffle walls to protect against artillery shrapnel and splinters. For concealment, the structure was covered with a thin layer of earth and blended into the surrounding terrain and, if located in a trench line, the rear side was flush with the trench wall. For defence and observation of the battle zone, the shelter had a concrete fire step (2). Steel hand rungs (3) were set into the rear wall to help soldiers get into action rapidly. Most front lines had some means of

observation such as a hole for a periscope or a sentry pit so that the occupants could watch for an Allied infantry attack. The shelter's interior was a single, cramped room accommodating four to six soldiers. Inside height was about 4 feet (1.5m), too low for the soldiers to stand upright. To prevent concrete spalling when hit by an artillery round, the ceiling was lined with sheets of corrugated iron. Shelters located rear of the forward trenches were more spacious and had two or more rooms furnished with bunk beds, shelves, tables and chairs. The designs were also more varied and elaborate with better ventilation, lighting, heating and drainage, along with additional features such as conduits for telephone wires. The entrances were sometimes equipped with thick wooden doors reinforced with sheet iron plates.

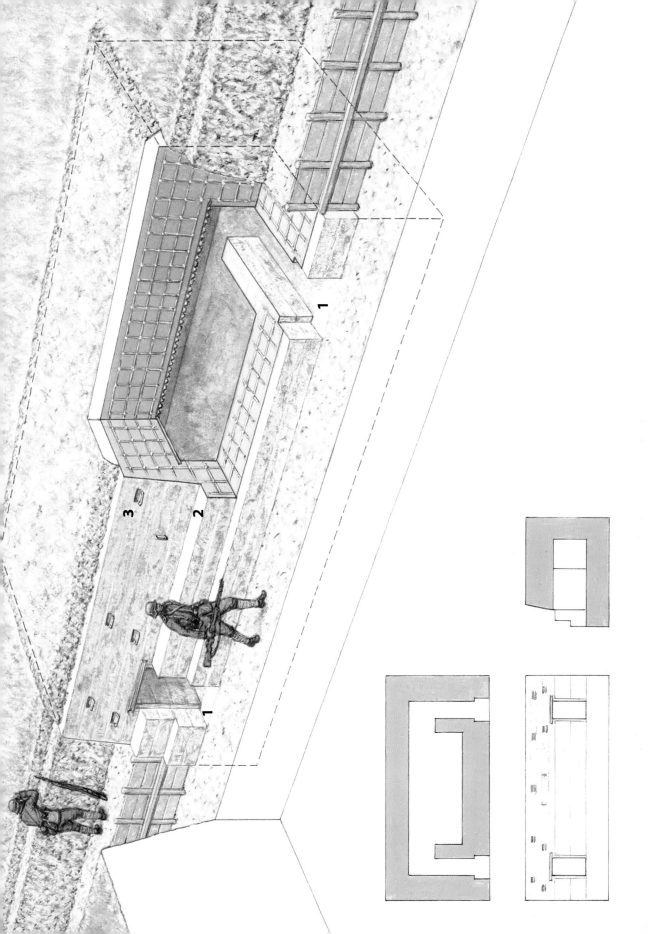

The barbed wire in the entanglements was arranged in a random manner that did not follow any uniform system and was loosely strung so that it could absorb shellfire. The pickets were spaced on average 6.5 feet (2m) apart and were made of either wood or metal. Gaps were left in the entanglements located behind the forward trenches to allow the passage of troops. To conceal these gaps from enemy observation, they were formed into a blind by overlapping lengths of entanglements. Wide gaps were created by emplacing pickets without wire and then leaving sufficient wire nearby to close the gap when necessary. Narrow gaps were closed with portable wire obstacles. These types of obstacles had many forms, which included wood or metal frames strung with barbed wire, sometimes called *chevaux-de-frise* or 'knife rests' (owing to their resemblance to now-antiquated tableware), expandable coils of wire and a portable unfolding barbed-wire, net-like contraption called the Lochmann entanglement. Other portable entanglements, or specially constructed wire gates, were used to block trenches from infiltration by enemy soldiers.

By doctrine, units were not to waste time and resources building revetments. However, this unusual photograph shows that the walls of this long-occupied Kriemhild-Stellung trench were reinforced with a combination of concrete, masonry and brushwood wattle. (NARA)

## Trenches

Forward of the main entanglement belts were the outpost zone earthworks. These positions consisted of one or two lines of rudimentary trenches and foxholes, backed up by squad-sized battle positions. Behind the outpost zone was the trench system of the main line of resistance. Further to the rear, perhaps as far as 1.5 miles (2.5km), was a second trench system known as the artillery protective line (called the reserve line by the Allies). The distance between the two trench systems was meant to delay the advance of any Allied force that breached the first trench lines by forcing the assaulting infantry to wait until artillery moved forward for the assault on the second trench system. Both trench systems consisted of two, sometimes three, lines of trenches, laid out in irregular, broken parallel lines. If only two trench lines were dug, then the forward-most trench served as the front-line combat position, while the second trench line served as a secondary line of defence and a support or circulation trench that soldiers used to move and reposition themselves along the front. If a third trench was dug, then the first trench line was often used primarily as an observation position. The trench lines were spaced several hundred yards apart so all trenches could not come under artillery fire simultaneously, yet were still close enough that units could rapidly respond to an Allied attack. Trench lines zigzagged across the battle zone to take advantage of the terrain and were often located on a reverse slope of a hill. This greatly limited the fields of fire of the German infantry and machine guns, but offered significant protection from Allied artillery. Emplacements for machine guns, anti-tank rifles, field and anti-aircraft guns

First-line shelters were designed to protect soldiers from artillery bombardment and serve as a fighting position. Chunks of moss camouflaged this Kriemhild-Stellung shelter's facade, which featured inset handholds and a fire step. German soldiers added a gas alarm and directional sign above the roofline. (NARA)

and trench mortars were either dug directly into the trench lines or connected via saps (short narrow trenches).

The form of the trench lines varied considerably according to function and the nature of the ground. Firing or fighting trenches – *Schützengräben* – ideally consisted of a series of alternating fire-bays and traverses to limit the effect of enemy enfilade fire (i.e. fire along the length of the trench) or shellfire. The front side of a fighting trench had earthen parapets to provide cover for soldiers while they were firing at the enemy and an earthen mound – called a parados – on the rear side to protect against shells bursting behind the trench. To prevent easy detection by assaulting Allied troops, parapets and parados were generally no more than a foot and a half above ground, although in rocky, hard or swampy ground, where trenches could not be dug deeply, the parapets and parados had to be significantly raised above ground level. Trenches were dug wider at the top than at the bottom, creating a 'V' shape that allowed trench walls to stand without revetment and reduced the likelihood of the trench being blocked by shellfire. Experience on the Somme

Interiors of concrete shelters in forward areas were sparse with no built-in comforts. To prevent spalling if hit by artillery, the shelter's ceiling and one wall were lined with sheets of corrugated iron. (NARA)

showed that deep, narrow trenches too often collapsed under artillery fire, burying soldiers and hindering movement through the trench systems. The width and depth of trenches varied greatly. Front-line trenches were about 11 feet (3.5m) wide at the top, 3 feet (1m) wide at the bottom, and 6 feet (2m) deep, which was sufficient to protect soldiers moving along the trench. To facilitate firing and observation, the front side of the trench often had a fire step. Trenches in the rear, such as the artillery protective line, were simpler, often lacking a fire step, and shallower, perhaps only 8 feet (2.5m) wide and 5 feet (1.5m) deep.

Communication trenches connected the fighting trenches and earthworks into a network that permitted troops to move around the battle zone without exposing themselves to small-arms or artillery fire. The trenches generally ran perpendicular

During postwar surveys of German defences, Allied troops encountered many types of shelters. This Michel-Stellung command post was dug into the reverse slope of a steep hill and camouflaged with brush hurdles. Windows provided light and ventilation for the headquarters' staff and could be shuttered if the shelter came under fire. (NARA)

to the front line in long curves or zigzags, except when close to the front line where traverses were needed to protect against enfilading fire. Communication trenches were narrower and shallower than fighting trenches. Where a communication trench intersected a front-line trench, the junction was often constructed as a strongpoint. Communication trenches were more numerous in forward areas close to the front line than in rear defensive portions. A typical company sector had two communication trenches or, on average, one every 300 yards (275m). Some communication trenches – called switch trenches – were built to serve as fighting trenches so that Allied infantry in the battle zone could be trapped in a pocket and exposed to fire on three sides. Switch trenches resembled fighting trenches in form, although they were often simpler in construction.

After 1916, trenches were not routinely reinforced with revetments unless soil conditions made it necessary to keep the walls from collapsing. Revetted trenches were most common in the wet ground of Flanders and the Somme. Revetments were made from a variety of materials including wire mesh, planks, brush, concrete and even brick or masonry (especially in the Argonne region of the Kriemhild-Stellung). Narrow communication trenches were sometimes braced with overhead struts to strengthen the revetments. Great effort was put

## E ANTI-TANK MINEFIELDS

The Allies' successful use of tanks prompted the German Army to make and employ anti-tank mines. In some sections of the Siegfried defences, long lines of mines were emplaced several hundred yards forward of the wire entanglements belts to incapacitate or destroy tanks before they could reach the trench lines. Additional minefields were sometimes emplaced in and behind the main line of resistance and integrated with barricades to form an in-depth tank defence. Some minefields were several miles long and contained several thousand mines. Mines were typically emplaced at intervals of 6–10 feet (2–3m) in lines, or checkerboard patterns. Wire entanglements were frequently emplaced over the minefields to conceal them from Allied observation or mark their location to defending troops.

A variety of mine types within the same minefield was common. The earliest and simplest minefields consisted of 150mm or 210mm high-explosive artillery shells equipped with a standard percussion fuse or a spring detonator, buried vertically in the ground (1). A later version consisted of a wooden box containing one or more artillery shells laid horizontality in the box (2). The detonating device was a spring-fuse lighter set to detonate under a under a heavy weight of 450kg (1000lb) or more. The mines were wrapped in tar paper for water resistance and placed in a shallow hole with the top of the box just below ground surface. More sophisticated mines consisted of 6.5lb (5kg) or more of high explosive in a wood or metal box (3 & 4) equipped with multiple spring-fuse lighters or firing pins.

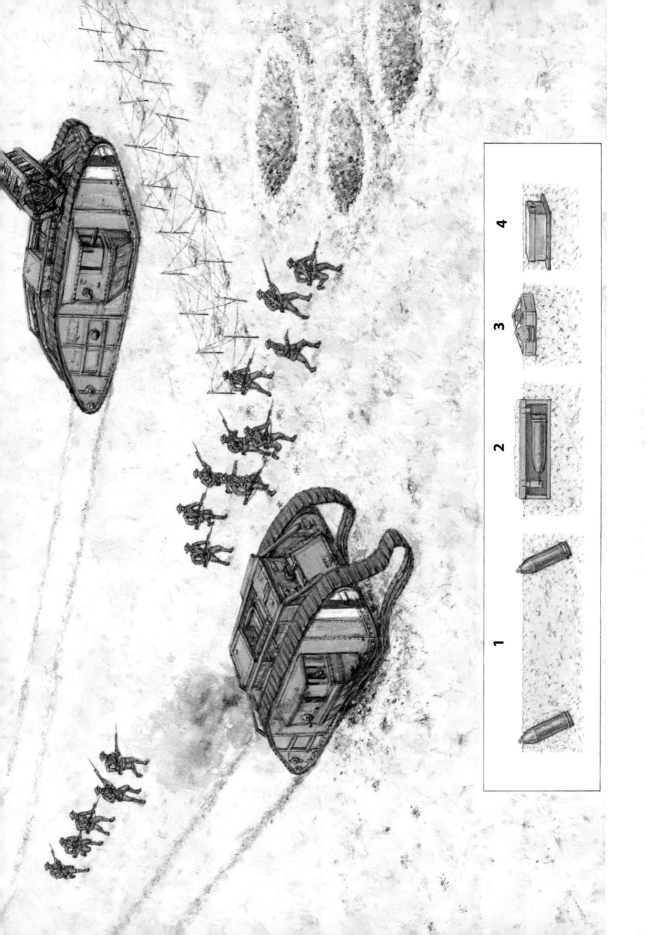

into keeping the trenches dry. Elaborate drainage systems of ditches, pipes and sumps with hand pumps were commonplace. However, unless a trench was prone to flooding, wooden flooring (i.e. duck boards) was not widely used except at the entrances to shelters and dugouts. Latrines, an important part of trench life, were sited off main trenches and connected by saps.

## Concrete shelters

The German Army built many more concrete fortifications than the Allied armies. The use of concrete began in mid-1915 when earth and timber shelters were strengthened with concrete roofs supported by joists of iron rails. However, these shelters could not stand up to artillery fire and were replaced in 1916 by shelters made of either poured concrete or pre-cast concrete block reinforced with iron rods. However, while these structures were significantly stronger, they could still be destroyed by a direct hit from heavy artillery and did not adequately protect occupants from the concussive effects of a near miss. Thus, for the Siegfried positions, even stronger shelters made of concrete reinforced with iron rods were built to replace the older poured concrete and block structures, although concrete block construction continued in forward areas where building with reinforced concrete was impractical because of the proximity to Allied lines. The new shelters were designated as *Mannschafts-Eisenbeton-Unterstände* or 'MEBU' (reinforced concrete shelters for troops). The primary purpose of these shelters was to protect soldiers from Allied artillery bombardment. However, other shelters were designed and built to also function as machine gun emplacements, observation posts, command posts, communication centres and medical aid stations. These specialized shelters were intermixed with the troop shelters. In most sectors, MEBU were built below ground level using cut and fill construction techniques. If the water table or soil conditions did not allow such construction (such as in Flanders), then the shelters were built above ground and camouflaged by earth and vegetation, or built inside a building. British soldiers nicknamed these surface shelters 'pillboxes' in 1917, and the British built many of their own after closely examining German types.

The size and design of the shelters varied depending on their location in the defensive zone. Shelters located in the main line of resistance were small structures designed to withstand direct hits by 6in (150mm) shells. For

This machine-gun emplacement was sited to protect a road near Thiaucourt in the Michel-Stellung. The high water table of the Woëvre plain likely required that the shelter be built above ground. For protection against artillery fire, additional concrete was added to the roof. (NARA)

This Wotan-Stellung machine-gun emplacement near La Bassée is set well above ground level owing to the high Flanders water table. A thick concrete roof and walls provided blast protection, whilst a layer of turf provided a modicum of camouflage. (NARA)

concealment, the shelters were covered with a thin layer of earth and blended into the surroundings. Each shelter had a single room to accommodate four to six soldiers. Most front-line shelters were equipped with some means of observation, such as a hole for a periscope or a sentry pit so that occupants could watch for an Allied infantry attack, and a fire step so that they could serve as fighting positions. Sufficient shelters were built to accommodate all soldiers manning the front line. In densely fortified areas, shelters were placed as close together as every 55–110 yards (50–100m). Larger shelters for reserve units were located further back in the battle zone. In between the main line of resistance and the artillery protective line, the shelters could accommodate up to half a platoon or two squads (12–24 soldiers). Compared to the front-line shelters, the interiors were more spacious, with two or more rooms. Shelter designs were also more varied and elaborate with better ventilation, lighting, heating and drainage along with additional features such as conduits for telephone wires. Some of the shelters had fire steps for defence and for direct observation of the battle zone. For purposes of command and control, the shelters were grouped into company-sized positions around command posts. Even larger shelters for a platoon or more of battalion reserve troops were positioned within and behind the artillery protective line. These rear-area shelters were bombproof against up to 11-inch (270mm) heavy artillery rounds and when possible were positioned on reverse slopes, in woods and in ravines.

Several types of concrete shelter were designed to serve as machine-gun positions. However, for survivability, especially in forward areas, machine guns generally operated from open field emplacements that were easy to conceal from aerial and ground observation. To speed getting a machine gun into action, the gun and ammunition were stored in recesses built into the firing emplacement while the crew used a nearby concrete shelter. The field positions were either built into the trench lines or placed in front of or behind a trench and connected by a sap or tunnel. Behind forward trenches, concrete shelters were built as hardened machine-gun emplacements. These shelters could only be partially buried because siting the machine gun embrasures at ground level left the top half the shelters exposed above ground. This problem was partially solved by concealing the machine-gun shelters in villages, farms or woods.

The Germans preferred to establish command posts in shelters rather than caves or dugouts.

This shelter for a trench mortar and crew in the Kriemhild-Stellung did not provide much protection against heavy artillery fire, but it could have resisted light artillery rounds and rifle grenades. Foliage made it difficult for American troops to locate it in the autumn of 1918. (NARA)

If possible, command shelters were sited on the reverse slopes of hills located behind the front lines at a distance no further back than the length of front held by that unit. For example, shelters for company headquarters were located 100 yards (90m) or so behind the main trench line, while battalion command shelters were about 1,000 yards (900m) to the rear, and shelters for the regiments' headquarters were some 2,200 yards (2,000m) away from the front line. Forward command posts for company and battalion headquarters were built according to a standard design and from the outside looked much liked any other shelter. However, in contrast to troop shelters, command shelters were larger and had better lighting, ventilation and heating to facilitate the work of the staff. Further to the rear, shelters for regiment and division headquarters were more elaborate, and adapted to the needs of the larger staffs. For communications, a network of buried telephone cables connected the various command posts.

Telephone was the primary means of communication in the fortified positions. Cables were buried in deep trenches, and concrete shelters were built as communication centres to house 'telephone parties' for testing and maintaining the telephone lines. (NARA)

40

## Dugouts

Construction and use of dugouts by the German Army long pre-dated the creation of the Siegfried positions. The first dugouts were shallow holes excavated into the sides of trenches, but as the intensity of Allied artillery fire increased, the dugouts went deeper underground and grew in size to accommodate more soldiers. However, the use of dugouts was problematic because soldiers often had insufficient time to reach the surface between the end of an Allied barrage and the beginning of a troop assault, causing them to be killed or captured as they emerged from the dugouts. Furthermore, Allied heavy artillery could collapse dugout entrances and trap the occupants underground. For these reasons, in 1916 the army prohibited dugouts in forward areas and replaced them with concrete shelters, although construction of deep dugouts in the rear areas continued. Depending on topography and geological conditions, dugouts varied in size and form, from small, single-chamber dugouts for a few soldiers, to large multi-level excavations for entire units. The depth to which dugouts were excavated was governed by ground-water level, but at least 33 feet (10m) overhead cover in solid subsoil and 16 feet (5m) in rock was thought sufficient to protect against the heaviest artillery fire. Entrances to dugouts located on reverse slopes had horizontal galleries tunnelled on a slightly rising grade to facilitate drainage, while dugouts in open or rolling terrain had entrances dug on a descending incline at about 45 degrees. Reinforced concrete, steel beams or sheets of corrugated iron were used to strengthen dugout entrances against artillery fire. The interiors were braced with timber frameworks and lined with wooden planks. Most dugouts were equipped with electric lights, heating, ventilation, drainage systems and furniture such as beds, chairs, tables and shelves. Large dugouts often had two levels, or floors, with the top floor serving as living quarters and the lower floor as a deeper refuge during intense bombardment. Generally, dugouts had two entrances separated by at least 50 feet (15m).

Forward observation posts were sometimes improvised from whatever materials were available. Resembling a Samurai helmet, this unusual example was made of heavy steel plate capped with concrete to deflect incoming rounds. (NARA)

Various types of concrete shelters were built in the rear areas to protect against Allied long-range shelling. This shelter in an engineer depot has thick walls and an angled roof shaped to prevent penetration by a direct hit. (NARA)

## Artillery positions

During the artillery battles of 1916 at Verdun and the Somme, the German Army stopped building shelters for artillery pieces after finding that guns placed in them were easily detected and destroyed by Allied artillery. As an alternative, the artillery turned to mobility and concealment for survivability. Thus, in contrast to the elaborate concrete shellproof shelters built for infantry units, artillery and trench mortar batteries were emplaced in open earthworks. Field-gun emplacements were dug so that the guns had a wide field of fire while trench mortars were emplaced in simple pits. Sometimes shallow dugouts with splinter-proof cover or cut-and-cover shelters were provided for the crews and munitions. Multiple emplacements were prepared so that the guns and mortars could frequently move to alternative positions. Larger-calibre indirect-fire artillery was located well to the rear, behind the second trench system, yet close enough to the front lines so that the guns could concentrate fire on an Allied attack. Emplacements for the guns were little more than a level spot on the ground. Within a battery position, trenches and timber-frame shelters covered with corrugated iron and earth were sometimes built to protect the crews and munitions. Anti-aircraft guns were also emplaced in simple earthworks, although concrete shelters were built to house searchlights.

Observation posts for commanders and artillery observers were sited to overlook the outpost and battle zones. In forward areas, the posts were small, ground-level structures, often little more than an earthwork position built into a trench. To provide additional protection, some forward observation posts were hardened with one of several types of pre-fabricated steel plate structures that were set in concrete, covered with a layer of concrete several feet thick, and then camouflaged with earth. Behind the trenches of the main line of resistance, larger and more elaborate observation posts were emplaced on high ground. These posts were often reinforced concrete shelters topped by an armoured cupola. Further to the rear, in the vicinity of the artillery positions, observation towers as much as 80 feet (25m) tall were built to gain a viewpoint behind Allied lines. Most towers were timber-frame constructions, although in the Flandern and Wotan positions, several large concrete observation towers were built and camouflaged as buildings. In wooded areas, such as the Argonne, observation towers were often built into the trees.

This tank barrier shielding a vulnerable stretch of the Drocourt–Quéant Switch (Wotan-Stellung) near Cambrai was comprised of 6-inch steel L-beams. Spacing was narrow enough to prevent passage by Renault FT light tanks, which were 5.5 feet (1.7m) wide. (NARA)

Rolling Barricade - near Sponville

11-21-18

## Tank defences

The German Army began building anti-tank obstacles into the Siegfried positions in 1918. The purpose of these was to slow the advance of tanks and channel them into the fire of field guns or heavy artillery. The obstacles were arrayed in multiple lines of defence along likely approaches such as broad fields, valley bottoms and roads. Gaps were left in the obstacle lines to allow movement of their own troops through the battle zone. To the Allies, the presence of anti-tank defences indicated the Germans had assumed a defensive posture and had little intention of going over to the offensive in that sector. With no set design, anti-tank obstacles were improvised constructions made by troops using locally available materials. The three basic types were ditches, barricades and minefields. Anti-tank

This unique Michel-Stellung barrier featured a modified mine car loaded with timbers encased in concrete and secured in place with 7-inch I-beams. When a wire cable that held the car to a tree was cut, the barrier would move into the concrete block on the left. (NARA)

German troops emplacing box and artillery shell mines during training, possibly at the training and mine testing ground near Briey, France. (NARA)

43

ditches were dug forward of the fighting trenches and were occasionally created by deepening and widening an existing trench line. The ditches were usually dug 6 feet (2m) deep with the soil mounded on either side to increase the depth of the ditch to 10 feet (3m). Occasionally, ditches were filled with water or had mines placed in the bottom. In open fields, lines of anti-tank barricades were sited in front of entanglement belts to separate tanks from infantry. The barricades were constructed of steel L-beams set 10 feet (3m) into the ground and spaced to prevent the passage of a tank or heavy artillery piece. The girders stood at least 6 feet (2m) above ground. The most common type of road barrier consisted of rows of reinforced concrete posts, steel girders or even wooden posts set into concrete. Another style of barricade consisted of logs bound together with cable and stacked between steel girders set vertically in concrete and bound together with cable. In village streets, barricades took many forms from well-constructed masonry walls to ad hoc piles of farm wagons and implements such as ploughs and harrows. Passage through road and street barricades was allowed by either building a chicane into the obstacle or leaving a gap that could be quickly barred using steel L-beams.

In mid-1918, the German Army employed anti-tank mines. The mines were designed to detonate under the weight of a tank and were emplaced in lines up to 2–3 miles (about 3–5km) in length. A single minefield could contain 7,000 mines. Minefields were generally placed forward of the first belt of wire entanglements in the outpost zone. To add depth to anti-tank defences, additional minefields were also emplaced further back in the battle zone in combination with other obstacles. The manufacture and emplacement of mines was not standardized and was still in a state of development when the war ended. The simplest mines were 150mm (6 inch), 210mm (8.3 inch) calibre high-explosive artillery shells buried directly into the ground. More commonly, one or two artillery shells were placed in a wooden box equipped with a detonating device. A more sophisticated type of mine was a wooden or metal box containing up to 11lbs (5kg) of perdite explosive and equipped with some type of spring or friction fuse lighter. The army also produced anti-personnel mines of a similar design containing a smaller perdite charge, although their use was not widespread.

## TANK BARRICADES

The German Army built barricades to block or delay the advance of Allied tanks and separate them from infantry formations. Barricades were emplaced among the trenches of the main line of resistance lines to prevent Allied tanks from moving across the open ground and usually anchored by strong points on either flank. To increase effectiveness, field guns were dug into positions where they could engage Allied tanks trying to negotiate the tank barriers. wo of the most common forms of barricades built across open fields were rows of steel I-beams set deep into the ground and spaced less than the width of an Allied tank, and lines of large reinforced concrete piers joined by several heavy cables suspended between the piers. There was no set standard of construction and combinations of barriers types were common. Main roads and village streets received special attention and a wide variety of barricades were built to bar the passage of tanks and other vehicles. One style consisted of logs bound together with cable and stacked between steel girders set vertically in concrete (1). Passage was allowed by a narrow chicane through the log barriers. Another style of barrier was made of I-beams set closely in a double row inclined at an angle of 70 degrees towards the direction from which Allied tanks were expected (2). Less commonly, complex movable barriers were constructed from steel I-beams and heavy angle iron (3). Main roads were also blocked by short anti-tank ditches – called tank traps – dug across the road and then either filled with water or mined.

Concerned about the increasing number of Allied tanks, the German Army began emplacing anti-tank minefields in the summer of 1918. This line of anti-tank mines in the Michel-Stellung was surveyed and demilitarized by American engineers in January 1919. (NARA)

**RIGHT**
One advanced type of anti-tank mine consisted of a wooden box to which a metal firing bar with four legs was mounted. Under a tank's weight the firing bar activated four spring fuses connected to detonators embedded in 3kg of high-explosive perdite. (NARA)

**LEFT**
Large-calibre artillery shells were used in many types of anti-tank mines. One common version was made of a buried wooden box containing a 21cm high-explosive round; its lid was set on a pair of wires that would snap under a tank's weight activating the shell's fuse. (NARA)

## Camouflage

Great lengths were taken by the German Army to mitigate Allied ground and aerial observation of the fortified positions. Although most trenches and entanglement belts could not be hidden from aerial observation, simple measures such as cut vegetation or brush screens were used to conceal trenches and entanglements from ground-level observation. Therefore, camouflage and concealment focused primarily on shelters, dugouts and artillery positions. Shelters were concealed within the trench lines by building them at ground level and covering them with earth so that they looked liked part of the trench wall. The facades of the shelters were camouflaged with vegetation and the concrete was sometimes stippled to blend it into the natural surroundings. Above ground, shelters and emplacements were particularly difficult to hide. These works were camouflaged with piles of earth or brush laid against, or on, the shelter to break up its silhouette. Shelters were also built into existing buildings or made to look like a building. Artillery emplacements and other open earthworks were camouflaged with canvas netting or cut vegetation. Decoy trenches, earthworks and artillery positions with dummy guns were built to draw artillery fire away from real positions.

# OPERATIONAL HISTORY

## Cambrai

The first major Allied offensive against the fortifications of the withdrawal positions was conducted against the Siegfried-Stellung (Hindenburg Line) on 20 November 1917. In what became known as the first battle of Cambrai, six divisions of the British Third Army supported by tanks penetrated defences of the German Second Army, capturing part of the Siegfried-Stellung. The fortifications in the vicinity of Cambrai were amongst the strongest of any the German Army had

In late April 1917, the Australians were the first Allied troops to attack and capture part of a Siegfried fortified position. This concrete shelter located in the Wotan-Stellung south-east of Arras suffered only minor damage from artillery fire during the battle. (IWM)

built. There were two trench systems in the main line of resistance (designated Siegfried I) and an intermediate position about 1.5 miles (2.5km) behind it. Four miles (6.5km) behind Siegfried I the defences of Wotan II protected the western approaches to Cambrai while Siegfried II, located south-east of the city, was in the initial stages of construction and not ready for combat. For the first time, the British employed massed armour, with 376 new Mark IV heavy combat tanks leading the infantry attack (complemented by 100 additional supporting tanks). The lead tanks carried large chained brushwood 'fascines' which were used to bridge the German trenches. The attack was a complete surprise and Crown Prince Rupprecht expressed alarm at how easily the tanks brushed aside the deepest barbed-wire belts, permitting infantry to not only break through Siegfried I and the intermediate line but to pierce Siegfried II. By evening about 4 miles (6.4km) of the Siegfried-Stellung Line had fallen, but the attack stalled because German artillery destroyed dozens of tanks. Several near Flesquières were taken out by the 54th Infantry Division's Field Artillery Regiment 108, Germany's best anti-tank formation. The German Second Army launched a textbook enveloping counter-attack on 30 December, retaking most of the ground lost to the Allies by 5 December. The Siegfried-Stellung had held, but more because of German tactics than its defences. (See Osprey Campaign Series 187: *Cambrai 1917: The Birth of Armoured Warfare*.)

First employed by German troops during the battle of Somme, these portable Lochmann wire entanglements were widely used in the Siegfried fortified positions to fill breaches in the wire defences or erect new entanglements to impede an Allied breakthrough. (NARA)

# Major Allied attacks against the Hindenburg Line, 1917–18

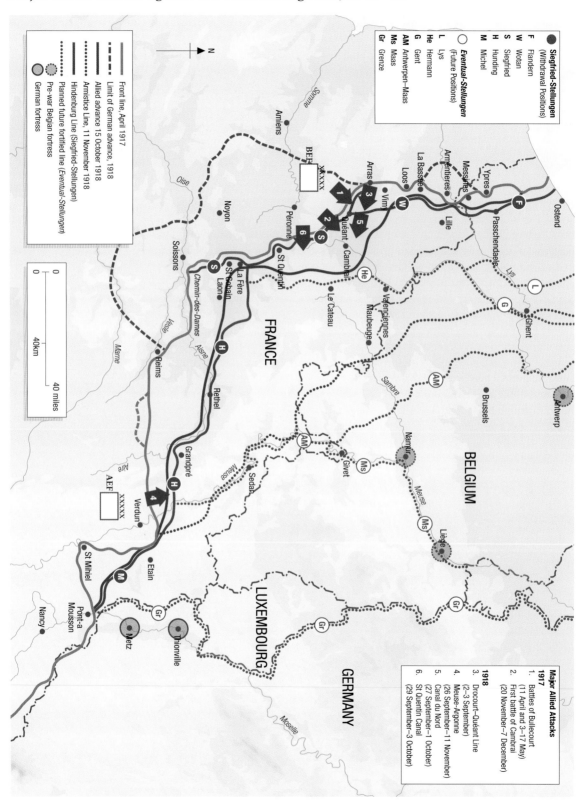

**Siegfried-Stellungen**
(Withdrawal Positions)

- **F** Flandern
- **W** Wotan
- **S** Siegfried
- **H** Hunding
- **M** Michel

**Eventual-Stellungen**
(Future Positions)

- **L** Lys
- **He** Hermann
- **G** Gent
- **AM** Antwerpen–Maas
- **Ms** Maas
- **Gr** Grenze

Front line, April 1917
Limit of German advance, 1918
Allied advance 15 October 1918
Armistice Line, 11 November 1918
Hindenburg Line (Siegfried-Stellungen)
Planned future fortified line (Eventual-Stellungen)
Pre-war Belgian fortress
German fortress

N

0
0
40km
40 miles

**Major Allied Attacks**

**1917**
1. Battles of Bullecourt
   (11 April and 3–17 May)
2. First battle of Cambrai
   (20 November–7 December)

**1918**
3. Drocourt–Quéant Line
   (2–3 September)
4. Meuse–Argonne
   (26 September–11 November)
5. Canal du Nord
   (27 September–1 October)
6. St Quentin Canal
   (29 September–3 October)

FRANCE

BELGIUM

LUXEMBOURG

GERMANY

Amiens
Somme
Oise
Noyon
Péronne
Soissons
Aisne
Vesle
Marne
Reims
Chemin-des-Dames
La Fère
St Gobain
Laon
Rethel
Grandpré
Aire
Meuse
Verdun
St Mihiel
Étain
Pont-a-Mousson
Nancy
Metz
Thionville
Moselle
Sedan
Givet
Sambre
Maubeuge
Valenciennes
Le Cateau
St Quentin
Cambrai
Quéant
Lille
Vimy
Loos
La Bassée
Arras
Armentières
Messines
Ypres
Passchendaele
Ostend
Lys
Ghent
Brussels
Namur
Liège
Antwerp

BEF
XXXXX

AEF
XXXXX

**1** **2** **3** **5** **6** **4**

**S** **H** **M** **W** **F** **L** **G** **He** **AM** **Ms** **Gr**

On 11 November 1917, as the third battle of Ypres ended and the British prepared to attack at Cambrai, OHL had decided to launch a major offensive on the Western Front using reinforcements from the East to defeat the French and British armies before American forces could arrive in strength. In a series of five large-scale offensives commencing on 21 March 1918, the German Army broke through Allied lines, made deep advances and inflicted a large number of casualties on the Allies, even getting close enough to Paris to shell the city with long-range artillery. However, the Allied armies did not collapse and the Germans' final offensive, named *Friedensturm* (peace offensive), launched in July near the city of Reims quickly disintegrated when counter-attacked by four French armies reinforced by eight fresh American divisions. Ominously, from March to July the German Army suffered a million casualties while Allied strength increased with the arrival of American troops. Exhausted, the German Army could no longer execute large-scale attacks or hold on to its gains, and the initiative on the Western Front passed to the Allies. Lossberg, still serving as chief of staff of the Fourth Army, recommended abandoning territory conquered since March and returning to the security of the fortifications of the old front lines, especially the Wotan and Siegfried positions, but Ludendorff refused.

Men of the 5th Australian Division advancing across country from their assembly area near Hesbecourt on their way to attack the Siegfried-Stellung on 29 September 1918. They are passing 8th Battalion, Tank Corps, Mark V tanks equipped with trench-crossing 'cribs' near Bellicourt. (IWM)

## Hamel

Just before Ludendorff's final offensive, a minor Allied attack conducted on 4 July about 9 miles (14km) east of Amiens against the German Second Army foreshadowed Allied tactics in coming battles. The battle of Hamel, carried out by the Australian Corps of the British Fourth Army, featured the debut of 60 heavy Mark V tanks and, for the first time in the British Army, aircraft in direct support of tanks – a practice initiated by the French Army in May 1917. The aircraft, from No. 8 Squadron of the Royal Air Force, relayed information about the tanks' progress, attacked German field guns and even provided air supply by parachuting small-arms ammunition and medical supplies to front-line troops. In a very brief but important battle, Australian and American troops seized Hamel ridge and successfully employed combined-arms tactics against entrenched German infantry. Various measures were implemented to deceive the Germans into believing no attack was in the offing, including forsaking a conventional artillery preparation; instead, the entire force attacked simultaneously at dawn, taking the defenders by surprise. German soldiers were also tricked into donning gas masks through the clever use of smoke shells. Although small, Hamel marked a high point in World War I combined-arms assault methods.

German gunners in full kit training to knock out tanks with a Skoda 7.5cm Model 15 infantry gun in September 1918. (NARA)

## Amiens

The tactics at Hamel were successfully repeated on a far larger scale a month later on 8 August when the British Fourth and French First armies again attacked the German Second Army east of Amiens. In what was a turning point in the war, Allied armies employed more than 500 tanks and armoured cars – the largest concentration of the war – to inflict severe losses of men and material on the German Army. As at Hamel, there was no tell-tale lengthy artillery preparation, low-flying aircraft were used to mask tank noise and the entire force moved forward before dawn. The assault's sudden ferocity shattered the German defences as counter-battery fire, greatly facilitated by aerial reconnaissance, devastated German artillery positions. The Allies penetrated German defences as aircraft opened the way for the tanks by attacking German anti-tank guns. Cavalry and armoured cars then moved forward, continued the advance, and with aircraft support prevented German units from rallying as retreating troops fell back on their own lines of communication and became entangled with reserves moving forward. The offensive petered out by 11 August, but the Allies had advanced as deep as 7.5 miles (12km), initiating three months of semi-mobile warfare on the Western Front. In retrospect, the British identified 8 August as the beginning of the 'Hundred Days', culminating in the 11 November Armistice.

Amiens badly shook OHL's confidence in their soldiers' morale and Ludendorff, because troops were surrendering en masse, famously described the first day of the battle as 'the black day of the German Army'. Annoyed by Crown Prince Rupprecht's desire to withdraw in the face of renewed attacks, on 12 August Ludendorff stripped the Second Army from his command and placed it with the Eighteenth and Ninth armies under the newly formed Army Group von Boehn, with Lossberg appointed chief of staff. Like Rupprecht, Lossberg pleaded with Ludendorff to pull back to the old front line, arguing that the Allies now had the initiative and reserves should not go to front-line units but instead be sent to build up and man the Siegfried defences. Ludendorff ignored all arguments and on 20 August the French Tenth Army attacked between Compiègne and Soissons (the Oise–Aisne Offensive) inflicting significant losses on the German Ninth Army, forcing it to withdraw between the Oise and the Ailette – an event Ludendorff identified as another black day. However bleak the situation appeared, Ludendorff remained hopeful that his armies would stiffen as they fell back on their final lines of defence.

## Drocourt–Quéant Line

The Allies soon renewed the offensive, advancing with five French and British armies along a broad front from Arras to Noyon. In the face of this onslaught, Ludendorff finally ordered a major withdrawal and the British First Army was able to push east of Arras towards the Wotan-Stellung, known as the Drocourt–Quéant Line by the British (who generally named German fortified positions after nearby towns). There, the German Seventeenth Army was holding a deep defensive zone that included the old British and German front-line positions (those built prior to the spring

A Flandern-Stellung machine-gun position and observation post built to resemble a small cottage, after having undergone very heavy bombardment, October 1918. (NARA)

offensives), several secondary switch positions, the heavily fortified Wotan-Stellung and the Canal du Nord, which the army intended to use as a ready-built anti-tank ditch. Even more defensive positions were planned behind the Wotan-Stellung, but they were little more than sketches on a map. OHL therefore knew that the loss of the Wotan position would not only threaten the critical logistical centre of Cambrai and the right flank of the Siegfried-Stellung, but could also result in an Allied breakout into open country and a collapse of the front.

Across the Western Front the German Army was losing ground to Allied attacks at an alarming rate. Worse still, casualties were high (228,000 soldiers in August) and more and more troops were simply surrendering (some 200,000 had been taken prisoner since July), while the army groups were receiving fewer than half as many replacements, many of whom were inexperienced and unreliable. Ludendorff's army group commanders pleaded with Ludendorff to authorize a general retreat to the Antwerpen–Maas Line, 70 miles (110km) to the east. Instead, Ludendorff chose a half-measure, a limited withdrawal of about 10 miles (6km) along a 55-mile (90km) frontage centred on the Second Army's front to the so-called Kanal-Stellung (canal position). This notional defensive line stood in front of the Somme's west bank, taking in the southern Canal du Nord winding from Noyon through Ham. The Seventeenth and Eighteenth armies completed their pullback even as the British First Army resumed its advance on Wotan.

Leading the First Army's attack was the Canadian Corps, reinforced by 23 artillery brigades. Its plan was to attack along the road from Arras to Cambrai, penetrating the German defences just north of where the Wotan and Siegfried positions met at Quéant. Early on 26 August, the artillery briefly, but fiercely, bombarded German positions, disorganizing the infantry and neutralizing the artillery. Even so, when the corps' three divisions attacked, they encountered numerous pockets of resistance and spent most of the day battering themselves against strongpoints equipped with machine guns. However, the Canadian Corps could not be stopped, and by day's end

British infantry marching down a sunken road in the Siegfried-Stellung near Bellicourt immediately after the battle of the St Quentin Canal on 4 October 1918. The barbed-wire entanglement has been damaged by artillery fire. (IWM)

the infantry had advanced about 3 miles (5km). Several strong German counter-attacks failed, and during the next four days the Canadian Corps continued the advance along the Arras–Cambrai road, seizing a section of the Rouvroy–Fresnes–Boiry-Riegel (a support position to the old front line), reaching the forward edge of the Wotan-Stellung. The artillery relentlessly pounded German positions, firing some 10,000 tons of ammunition between 27 August and 1 September.

The First Army then assaulted the Wotan-Stellung on 2 September. The plan was for the Canadian Corps to attack on a narrow front centred on the Arras–Cambrai road, break into the fortification line and then roll back the northern and southern flanks of the penetration. As the First Army's main effort, the corps was assigned 31 artillery brigades for fire support, counter-battery fire and interdictory fire to prevent counter-attack formations from crossing the Canal du Nord. Two companies of Mark V tanks led each

## G  WEAPONS EMPLACEMENTS

Survivability of crew-served weapons in frontline positions was important to the designers of the Siegfried fortifications. Initial plans for concrete shelters included versions for accommodating machine guns, trench mortars and field guns. In the case of heavy machine guns (1), the shelters were designed to not only protect the soldiers and weapons from destruction during an artillery bombardment but also serve as hardened fighting positions for the weapons. However, to allow machine guns to fire from inside the shelter, the top-half of the shelters had to protrude almost 9 feet (3m) above ground level to permit clearance for the firing embrasures. This example built opposite French forces was large – approximately 26 feet (8m) long and 16 feet (5m) wide – with two rooms, one for to serve as the machine-gun firing position and another for the crew and their

equipment. The shelters' high profiles made them easy targets for Allied artillery observers and construction of these shelters was largely abandoned in favour of small concrete shelters for the crew located near earthen machine gun emplacements. Shelters for trench mortars and field guns (2) were built just below ground level and included entrances wide enough for the weapon to be pulled out of the shelter and quickly put into action. This field gun emplacement located opposite the British army had three rooms – one for the crew, the gun and a protective infantry detachment. Ammunition was stored in a pit under the gun. When called into action, the crew dropped the door of the shelter onto the ramp, rolled their field gun up the ramp onto the firing platform, and emplaced the gun using the top of the shelter for concealment and protection.

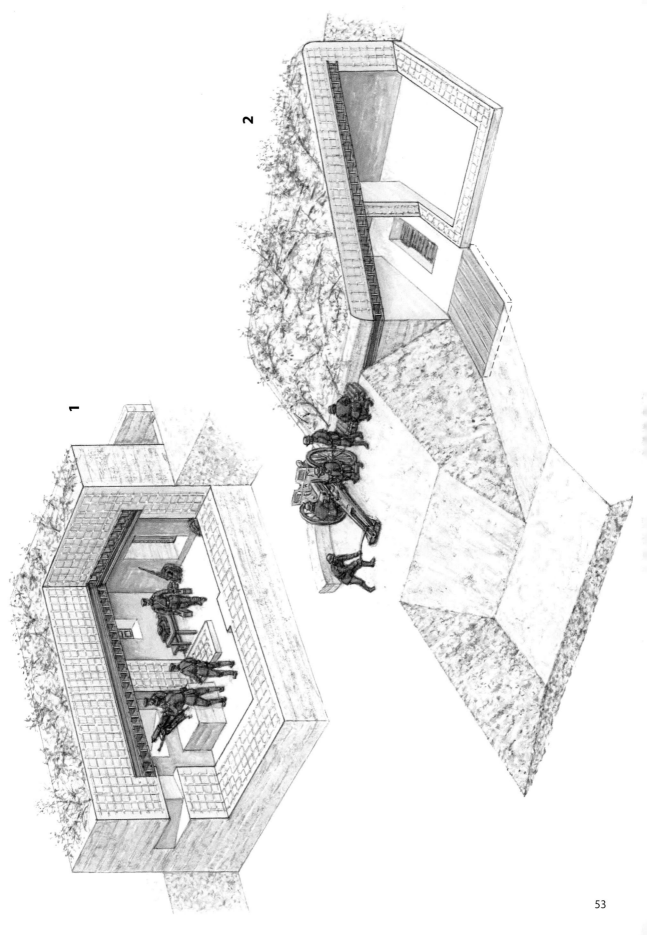

1

2

assault division, while RAF 1 Brigade provided air support. To safeguard the First Army's right flank, both the Third and Fourth armies would attack further south in the direction of the Siegfried-Stellung. Some 1.5 miles (2.5km) wide, the Wotan-Stellung occupied a series of shallow ridgelines with two main trench systems spaced about 200 yards apart protected by deep wire entanglements and dozens of concrete shelters. A support line was dug into the forward slope of a 65-foot-high (20m) prominence called Mont Dury alongside the Cambrai road. Just to reach Mont Dury, attacking troops would have to negotiate a dozen individual trench lines, and the hill itself was studded with machine guns positioned to sweep the entire area. These defences had such a formidable reputation that British Expeditionary Force commander-in-chief Field Marshal Douglas Haig learned he might be scapegoated if heavy casualties were incurred by attempting to take them; inflicting heavy casualties was precisely what the Wotan-Stellung was designed to do. Overwhelmed by the sudden firepower of the First Army attack, German resistance varied considerably and the Canadians took large numbers of unwounded prisoners, although several German divisions put up fierce resistance, especially the elite but well-worn 1st and 2nd Guards Divisions around Mont Dury. By evening the Canadian Corps made a 4-mile (6.5km) breach in the Wotan-Stellung, the first major crack in the Siegfried fortification system. Only the Canal du Nord and the unfinished defences of the Hagen-Stellung stood in the way of the British First Army and the open country beyond.

The success of the Canadian-led assaults, accompanied by the seizure of the city of Péronne on the Somme on 1 September, forced Ludendorff to abandon the canal position after less than a week. Although alarmed at the possibility of an Allied breakthrough, he would only approve small adjustments in the front. At noon on 2 September Ludendorff ordered the Seventeenth Army to retire behind the Sensée River and the Canal du Nord, the first step in a broad but shallow general withdrawal behind the so-called

Thousands of mines protected the Michel-Stellung. One such mine near Regniéville obliterated this Renault FT tank of the French 14th Light Tank Battalion, which was supporting the American 5th Division during the St Mihiel offensive. Both crewmen perished in the explosion. (NARA)

Winter-Linie (Winter Line). As much a hopeful concept as a prepared position, Ludendorff's Winter Line incorporated the Siegfried-Stellung and the 20-mile (32km) stretch of the Somme north of Ham, which had already been compromised by the loss of Péronne. The Second Army, on Below's left, pulled back next, followed by the Eighteenth Army to its left, and both were placed behind the Siegfried-Stellung. Further south, the Seventh Army pulled back from the Vesle behind the Aisne. In the north, the Germans vacated the Lys salient between Ypres and Lens – abandoning the last territory conquered in the March–April period as part of OHL's spring offensives.

An increasingly edgy Ludendorff belatedly introduced his army group commanders to the Hermann-Stellung. Knowing that Hermann existed only on paper, and that the Siegfried-Stellung's defences had deteriorated badly since spring, Lossberg argued that the latter should only act as a trigger for a general withdrawal to the Antwerpen–Maas-Stellung. In the meantime, as much materiel as possible should be pulled behind the Antwerpen–Maas-Stellung and the transportation network destroyed to slow the Allied advance. Unswayed, Ludendorff insisted on holding the Siegfried-Stellung.

## Canal du Nord

After a three-week pause to regroup, the British First Army resumed the offensive. In the army's path was the Canal du Nord, a 59-mile (95km) unfinished, partially flooded canal that ran north to south across its line of advance. Just beyond the canal were the defences of the Hagen-Stellung consisting of two trench systems with extensive wire entanglements between the Canal du Nord and the Canal de l'Escaut. Designated by the British as the Marquion and Marcoing Lines, eight divisions of the German Seventeenth Army held these defences. Bourlon Wood, a strongly fortified height similar to Mont Dury that had helped blunt the Cambrai offensive in November 1917, dominated the ground between them. The Canadian Corps, augmented with extra artillery and, very importantly, engineers who constructed bridges to span the Canal du Nord, conducted the attack. The Canadian Corps concentrated two divisions on a narrow 1.5-mile (2.5km) front opposite a dry stretch of the canal. After the two lead divisions crossed the canal, the corps' two other divisions followed to expand the attack frontage to 8.5 miles (13.5km). When the attack commenced on the morning of 27 September, the Seventeenth Army was not prepared for the intensity of the Allied bombardment, which pinned down defending troops and allowed Canadian infantry to easily cross the canal and roll up the Marquion Line by nightfall. In a complex fire-support plan, six of ten artillery brigades fired the initial supporting barrages while four displaced forward. When the latter emplaced to bombard the second line, two of the rear brigades continued firing while the other two advanced, and so on, 'leapfrogging' forward to maintain the barrage on German positions. In support of the advance, engineer companies cleared mines and removed obstacles, often in the midst of battle. Although Bourlon Wood fell to enveloping Canadian attacks, German resistance stiffened and five days' hard fighting ensued as German divisions counter-attacked to regain lost ground. RAF squadrons added air support, calling down artillery upon several German counter-attacks. Eventually, some 31 German divisions fought to prevent a breakthrough, but it was not enough to prevent the Canadian Corps from reaching Cambrai's western edge by 1 October. The Germans evacuated Cambrai eight days later.

## St Quentin Canal

Two days after the First Army crossed the Canal du Nord, the British Fourth Army attacked the Siegfried-Stellung just south of Cambrai. There, the German Second Army was occupying a defensive zone some 6 miles (10km) deep formed by two fortified positions: Siegfried I, which was the original Siegfried-Stellung position built in late 1916 and early 1917, and Siegfried II, which was an unfinished reserve position located about two miles (3km) behind Siegfried I. Even further east, OHL had planned a Siegfried III position. Siegfried I consisted of four trench systems: three in the main line of resistance and one in the artillery protective line. Intertwined with the trench systems was the St Quentin Canal that ran behind, and sometimes within, the main line of resistance. At the point of the British Fourth Army's coming attack lay the 3.5-mile (5.5km) long Bellicourt tunnel, which formed a broad land bridge over the canal. On each side of the tunnel, the canal had 60-foot-high (18m) embankments, making a long and formidable anti-tank ditch. Several villages, notably Le Catelet at the canal's northern exit, and Magny-la-Fosse to the south, were turned into fortified strongpoints. The artillery protective line was located behind the canal. Although the defences were formidable, they had suffered neglect while the Germans were on the offensive in the spring. Even worse for the German Second Army, in August the British had captured the canal defence plans.

The British Fourth Army attacked the Siegfried-Stellung on a 12-mile (19km) front with three corps. The Australian Corps, reinforced by the American II Corps and 90 tanks, undertook the main effort directed at the Bellicourt tunnel, while IX Corps and the Third Army's V Corps conducted supporting attacks on the southern and northern flanks, respectively. The American 27th and 30th Divisions were to lead the attack to breach the German main defensive line, cross over the Bellicourt tunnel and assault the artillery protective line (known by the Allies as Le Catelet–Nauroy Line). The Australian 3rd and 5th Divisions would then pass through the Americans and cross the canal to assault the unfinished Siegfried II (Beaurevoir Line) fortifications to complete the penetration of the Siegfried-Stellung. The British guns began their preparatory bombardment on 26 September, for the first time firing mustard gas shells to contaminate deep German shelters in and around the canal. Early on 29 September the American divisions joined the assault. In the north, owing to problems with the British artillery fire plan, the 27th Division encountered especially fierce resistance, so when the Australian 3rd Division attempted to leapfrog the Americans it became embroiled in fighting west of the canal. With most supporting tanks destroyed or disabled, including those of the US 301st Battalion which encountered the tank-killing German Field Artillery Regiment 108, the battle turned into a close-combat fight for individual strongpoints that lasted for three days. However, the American 30th Division in the south was more successful. By afternoon it had captured the fortified village of Bellicourt at the tunnel's southern entrance, and the Australian 5th Division moved forward to continue the attack; but the advance was hampered by lack of progress on the left flank.

The turning point of the battle occurred south of the Bellicourt tunnel when the British 137th Brigade from IX Corps' 46th (Midland) Division, using life belts and collapsible boats, conducted a daring canal crossing to seize Riqueval Bridge before the Germans could detonate pre-placed

demolition charges. This *coup de main* permitted IX Corps' two divisions to cross the canal and capture a 4-mile (6.5km) section of Siegfried-Stellung and threaten Siegfried II. By 2 October the German Second Army had lost a 10-mile (17km) section of Siegfried I, and thousands of soldiers, many of whom were all too eager to surrender, were taken prisoner. After a brief pause, British Fourth and First armies decisively broke though Siegfried II, forcing OHL to order a general withdrawal to the line of the Hermann-Stellung, a move executed between 9 and 11 October.

A typical small Michel-Stellung shelter with a simple brush camouflage covering that made it difficult for aerial reconnaissance or approaching infantry to spot and bring under effective artillery fire. Shelling often churned ground and created debris to further conceal German fighting positions. (NARA)

## Meuse-Argonne

The first major American offensive of the war was against the St Mihiel salient, south-east of Verdun. Originally, this assault was planned as part of a much larger operation to attack and capture the fortified city of Metz. However, to better employ the American Army in a front-wide offensive towards the vital railway centre at Mézières, the St Mihiel offensive was scaled back with the aim now being to eliminate the salient, after which the Americans were to redeploy for an attack in the Argonne region west of Verdun. Realizing the St Mihiel salient was indefensible and that an attack was likely, Ludendorff ordered Armee-Abteilung C (Army Detachment C) to abandon the salient and occupy the Michel-Stellung. The withdrawal began on 11 September, one day before the start of the American offensive and, ironically, two years after withdrawal from the salient was first considered by Ludendorff during the Cambrai conference in September 1916. Despite being one of the two withdrawal positions originally proposed by Ludendorff,

the Michel-Stellung defences were incomplete. Many, but not all, of the planned concrete shelters and wire entanglements were in place, but few trenches had been dug. Now, as Army Detachment C occupied the position, its divisions hurriedly constructed more trench lines and wire entanglements and, expecting that a large number of tanks would accompany an attack, they also planted thousands of anti-tank mines, dug anti-tank ditches and installed a variety of road blocks along obvious avenues of approach toward Metz. However, the Michel-Stellung was never put to the test. On 12 September, as the German troops were withdrawing, the US First Army, supported by the French II Corps, attacked into the salient and, encountering only minor resistance, cleared it within five days. American and French troops reached the forward edge of the Michel-Stellung, whereupon the offensive was halted.

The American Army then shifted focus to the Argonne region for an attack north towards Sedan and the main railway which was used by the Germans to supply their armies or, in case of defeat, could evacuate them. As the US First Army prepared for the offensive, several deception operations were conducted to trick OHL into thinking that the next American offensive would either be towards Metz or perhaps in southern Alsace near Belfort. Defending the Argonne region were under strength divisions of the German Third and Fifth armies dug into rugged terrain well suited for defence. Having occupied the area for four years, the German defences were well planned although, because it was a quiet sector, the fortifications had received few resources for construction. Nevertheless, behind the front line there was a series of three unfinished fortified positions, the Ekkehard, Giselher and finally the Kriemhild portion of the Hunding-Stellung, which together formed a 10-mile (16km) deep defensive zone. The Meuse-Argonne offensive began on 26 September, less than two weeks after the attack at St Mihiel ended. The US First Army supported by French forces attacked along a broad 19-mile (30km) front, expecting to encounter weak resistance and capture the Kriemhild-Stellung on the very first day. However, the First Army's attack stalled as German formations, skilfully using the rugged terrain, inflicted heavy casualties on several American divisions. German reserve divisions moved in to bolster the defence and mount counter-attacks, forcing the US First Army to conduct a number of costly frontal assaults in order to maintain its advance.

After three weeks of combat, the US First Army finally reached the Kriemhild-Stellung, and on 14 October, in terrible weather, three American divisions attacked a section of the position located on the Romagne Heights. The defences were built on the Côte Dame Marie, a steep ridgeline anchored by strongpoints containing hundreds of machine gun positions and supported by artillery. The attack, planned as a double envelopment with a diversionary frontal attack in the centre, quickly broke down with heavy casualties sustained by both sides. After four days of fighting, the Germans were forced out of the position and withdrew several miles to the line of the planned, but not built, Freya-Stellung, leaving the Kriemhild-Stellung in the possession of the US First Army. At the same time, the French Fourth Army continued attacking on the US First Army's left (west) flank, advancing through several unfinished German defensive positions up to the line of the Hunding-Stellung, which assisted the Americans in the Argonne by forcing the German Third Army to pull back to the Kriemhild-Stellung.

The German Army was compelled to retreat to the Hermann and Hunding positions, neither of which provided much defensive advantage other than to serve as a rally line. On 25 October, the British Fourth Army overran the Hermann-Stellung near Le Cateau and the following day French divisions seized portions of the Hunding-Stellung north of Reims. Ludendorff and Hindenburg ordered the armies to fight to the finish, but on 27 October Ludendorff was compelled to resign and on 31 October now-Major-General Lossberg was assigned as chief of staff of Army Group Duke Albrecht, then occupying fortified positions in Alsace and Lorraine. On 4 November Anglo-French forces crossed the Sambre–Oise Canal, destroying whatever remaining value Hunding had as a defensive position. The same day American forces occupied the heights above Sedan, severing the main rail line between Metz and Lille. With a critical evacuation route cut and no fortified positions except for the Belgian pre-war fortresses at Antwerp, Namur and Liège, the demoralized and broken German Army had nowhere to organize a defence to stop the Allies before the German border. A defeated Germany finally agreed to an Armistice on 11 November.

# AFTERMATH

The Siegfried-Stellung, or Hindenburg Line, symbolized the quandary in which Germany found itself on the Western Front in the second half of the war. On the one hand, it could not afford any more costly battles like Verdun or the Somme and needed the fortifications to even the military balance. On the other hand, once the United States entered the conflict, Germany could not win the war by merely occupying fortifications and keeping its army on the defensive. The original purpose of the Siegfried positions was to conserve German strength while inflicting unacceptable casualties upon the French and British armies, possibly forcing the Allies to negotiate a favourable peace treaty while Germany still occupied Belgium and northern France. To that end, OHL's best option may have been to continue strengthening the fortifications and not abandon them for a desperate offensive that was uncertain to deliver a knockout blow to the Allies. However, Germany did not have the resources to build an impregnable defensive front. After the initial round of construction that built the Siegfried and Wotan positions, the labour and materials needed to build new, and maintain existing, fortifications steadily decreased. Furthermore, the German Army was unable to realize the intended benefit of the fortifications. After withdrawing to the Siegfried-Stellung, casualties remained high throughout 1917 because OHL's defensive principles were unevenly applied and, perhaps more importantly, because Ludendorff was unwilling to authorize withdrawals before front-line units were depleted. Thus, at Arras in April and May 1917, German divisions steadfastly held long-established and often unfavourable trench lines instead of withdrawing to reserve positions or the better-sited fortifications of the Wotan-Stellung. During the ill-fated French Nivelle Offensive, front-line units employing the new defensive tactics devastated two French armies, but as the French continued the offensive, the German victory was diminished because Ludendorff would not allow German units to withdraw before they suffered significant casualties. Finally, the long, bloody third battle of Ypres cost the Germans dearly because, even with Lossberg directing the defence, the army could not pull back to escape British artillery fire. In all three battles, the Allies and Germans both suffered heavy casualties, but it was the Germans who could least afford the loss.

When American troops first appeared on the front in late October 1917, Ludendorff decided (ironically, on 11 November) to return to the offensive, believing the time was right to defeat the exhausted British Army and bring the weary French and inexperienced Americans to the negotiating table. The 1918 spring offensives had some success, bringing the German Army within artillery range of Paris, but fresh American divisions arrived on the battlefield, denying the Germans victory and sapping German morale. By the time it became necessary for the German Army to fall back to the Siegfried, Wotan and the other withdrawal positions, it was too weak and demoralized to properly defend them. The Allies, employing new combined-arms tactics and weapons, especially tanks, were able to nullify any advantages the fortifications provided to the German Army. Germany's last line of defence was a forlorn hope.

After the war, the German Army continued practising defensive methods similar to those developed during the Great War, with special emphasis placed on anti-tank warfare. Anticipating a new European conflict, in 1936 Adolf Hitler ordered the construction of a fortification system on Germany's border with France, Belgium and Holland called the Westwall (which, confusingly, the British dubbed the Siegfried Line). These new fortifications and defences confronted by Allied troops in Normandy and a host of other locations during the Second World War were strikingly similar to those of the Siegfried positions. However, the 1940s version of the Siegfried-Stellung

proved little more successful than its Great War antecedent and fell to combined Allied forces in 1945.

After the war, French farmers toiled to dismantle the defences of the Siegfried positions and clear the land for cultivation. In some cases the dislodged material was used to repair farm buildings. Many concrete shelters were destroyed by detonating excess munitions inside them, with the resulting debris often being used as road stone. In other instances, the shelters' stout construction made removal of the remnants impossible or prohibitively expensive and dangerous. Although a large percentage of the fortifications that appeared in early postwar guides have since disappeared, some concrete shelters can still be found today scattered around the countryside. A number of readily available travel guides for Western Front visitors feature the surviving German fortifications as tour stops.

Portents of the future: Mark IV tanks of the British 1st Tank Brigade parked close to an unfinished concrete shelter of the Siegfried-Stellung near Flesquières in November 1917. (IWM)

# BIBLIOGRAPHY

## Archival sources

National Archives and Records Administration, College Park, Maryland; Record Group 120, Records of the American Expeditionary Forces; Entry 1780, Historical Report of the Chief Engineer of the AEF, 1917–1919

## Published sources

Balck, Wilhelm (translated by Harry Bell), *Development of Tactics–World War,* The General Service Schools Press, Fort Leavenworth, KS (1922)

Blair, Dale, *The Battle of Bellicourt Tunnel: Tommies, Diggers and Doughboys on the Hindenburg Line, 1918,* Frontline Books, London (2011)

Boff, Jonathan, *Winning and Losing on the Western Front: The British Third Army and the Defeat of Germany in 1918*, Cambridge University Press, Cambridge and New York (2012)

Braim, Paul F., *The Test of Battle: The American Expeditionary Forces in the Meuse-Argonne Campaign*, White Mane Books, Shippensburg, Pennsylvania (1998)

Bull, Stephen, *German Assault Troops of the First World War:* Stosstrupptaktik – *The First Stormtroopers,* Spellmount, Stroud, Gloucestershire (2007)

Bull, Stephen, *World War I Trench Warfare (2): 1916–18* (Elite Series), Osprey Publishing, Oxford (2002)

Cook, Tim, *Shock Troops: Canadians Fighting the Great War, 1917–1918*, Vol. 2, Viking Canada, Toronto (2008)

Harris, J. P., with Barr, Niall, *Amiens to the Armistice: The BEF in the Hundred Days' Campaign, 8 August–11 November 1918*, Brassey's, London and Washington, DC (1998)

Oldham, Peter, *The Hindenburg Line* (Battleground Europe Series), Pen & Sword, Barnsley, South Yorkshire (1997)

Palazzo, Albert, *Seeking Victory on the Western Front: The British Army & Chemical Warfare in World War I*, University of Nebraska Press, Lincoln, Nebraska (2000)

Reichsarchiv. *Der Weltkrieg 1914 bis 1918*, XIV Band, *Die Kriegsführung an der Westfront im Jahre 1918*, E. S. Mittler und Sohn, Berlin (1944)

Zabecki, David T., *The German 1918 Offensives: A Case Study of the Operational Level of War*, Routledge, London and New York (2006)

# GLOSSARY

*Artillerieschutzstellung*    Artillery protective line, an area typically several hundred metres behind the *Hauptverteidigungslinie* (main line of resistance) manned by infantry and machine-gun units to protect artillery batteries in case of an Allied breakthrough.

*Eingreif*    Interference or intervention. A designation given to troops or units tasked with executing counter-attacks. Sometimes seen as *Eingriff*.

*Eventual-Stellungen*    Future defensive positions, either planned or built, that would serve as rallying positions if the army was pushed from the front line.

*Gegenangriff*    Counter-attack.

*Gegenstöß*    Immediate counter-attack.

*Hauptverteidigungslinie*    Main line of resistance. Typically the most fortified part of a defensive zone.

*Hinterhangstellung*    Reverse slope position located behind the crest of a hill out of view of the enemy.

*MEBU*    *Mannschafts-Eisenbeton-Unterstände*, reinforced concrete personnel shelters.

*Rückzugsstellungen*    Defensive positions located behind the front line for use in the event of a withdrawal.

*Schützengräben*    Trenches built to serve as fighting positions for infantry, usually by constructing a fire step on the side of the trench closest to the enemy.

*Sperrfeuer*    Artillery barrage in front of a defensive zone to block or hinder enemy penetration.

*Stellung(en)*    Fortified defensive position(s) built of earth and concrete fortifications.

*Stützpunkt(e)*    Strongpoint(s).

*Trichterstellung*    Shell-hole position.

*Zwischenstellung*    Intermediate line or intermediate position between the *Hauptverteidigungslinie* (main line of resistance) and the *Artillerieschutzstellung* (artillery protective line). Sometimes called a *Mittelstellung*, *Mittellinie* or *Zwischenlinie*.

# INDEX

Page numbers in **bold** refer to illustrations and their captions.